LEAVE NO DOUBT

LEAVE NO DOUBT

A CREDO FOR CHASING YOUR DREAMS

MIKE BABCOCK

WITH RICK LARSEN

McGill-Queen's University Press

Montreal & Kingston · London · Ithaca

ISBN 978-0-7735-4031-6 (cloth)
ISBN 978-0-7735-4476-5 (paper)
ISBN 978-0-7735-8679-6 (ePDF)
ISBN 978-0-7735-8680-2 (ePUB)

Legal deposit first quarter 2012
Bibliothèque nationale du Québec

Reprinted in 2012
First paperback edition 2014
Printed in Canada on acid-free paper that is 100% ancient
forest free (100% post-consumer recycled), processed chlorine free

McGill-Queen's University Press acknowledges the support of the
Canada Council for the Arts for our publishing program. We also
acknowledge the financial support of the Government of Canada
through the Canada Book Fund for our publishing activities.

Library and Archives Canada Cataloguing in Publication

Babcock, Mike, 1963–
Leave no doubt : a credo for chasing your dreams / Mike Babcock
with Rick Larsen.

ISBN 978-0-7735-4031-6 (cloth)
ISBN 978-0-7735-4476-5 (paper)
ISBN 978-0-7735-8679-6 (ePDF)
ISBN 978-0-7735-8680-2 (ePUB)

1. Self-actualization (Psychology) 2. Success. 3. Determination
(Personality trait) 4. Hockey teams–Canada. 5. Olympic Winter
Games (21st : 2010 : Vancouver, B.C.) I. Houghton-Larsen,
Rick II. Title.

BF637.S4B29 2012   158.1   C2011-908449-X

Designed and typeset by studio oneonone in Minion 10.5/14

Frontispiece: The Stanley Cup visits the Babcocks at our summer
cottage in Emma Lake, Saskatchewan. Hoisting the cup with your
family makes it even more special. (Courtesy of the author)

For our Moms

CONTENTS

FOREWORD
Scotty Bowman

I consider it both an honour and privilege to write the foreword to this insightful book, *Leave No Doubt*, detailing the preparation and experiences that culminated in a gold medal for Canada in ice hockey at the 2010 Winter Olympic Games in Vancouver.

Having known Mike Babcock for over ten years, I am truly amazed at the details and thought processes Mike chronicles in this book. Needless to say, I came to respect him for his intensity and his thoroughness. He takes the reader through his early days as a coach, with all the trials and tribulations he encountered. Mike would go on to become the only man to win a World Junior Hockey Championship, a World Hockey Championship, a Stanley Cup Championship, and an Olympic Gold Medal.

Mike and I share many of the same beliefs, not just about running a successful team, but also about enjoying strong family values. He firmly believes in giving back and so he volunteers his time to a number of causes. He is very loyal to his home province of Saskatchewan, and I was proud to be in Saskatoon in July 2010 when the city held an official Mike Babcock Day. About $250,000 was raised for the new children's hospital.

Mike came up through the ranks, like I did myself. Nothing was handed to him; he had to work hard. He's used to working under pressure. In this book Mike refers to a quotation I gave him about attitude. I did it because we share the same ideas on this. We both believe that to be a successful person, player, or a successful coach, attitude is important.

At the Vancouver Olympics he was admired not only by the players on Team Canada but by the other coaches too, and by the general manager, Steve Yzerman. There was the added pressure for Canada playing on home ice, and knowing that in the 2006 Olympics, Canada had not even reached the final four. Mike was well aware of the pressure, and he responded well. He had a strong sense of kinship with the whole team and the coaches.

Leading up to the Vancouver games, Mike demonstrates in this book a clear conception of what he wanted, a confidence that his goal could be attained, a focus on what it would take, a commitment to how important it was to Canada, a strong character to stay on a proper course, and an ability to enjoy the process along the way. In the process, he creates for us a valuable, practical framework for achieving success.

In bringing home the gold medal for Canada in 2010, along with his earlier achievements, he reached the top of the hockey universe. He has left us a wonderful legacy that will inspire and motivate others to do the same in their chosen professions.

TEAM CANADA, 2010

Ages and team affiliations are from February 2010

Management

Steve Yzerman, Executive Director (Vice-President, Detroit Red Wings)

Doug Armstrong, Associate Director (Director of Player Personnel, St. Louis Blues)

Ken Holland, Associate Director (Executive Vice-President and General Manager, Detroit Red Wings)

Kevin Lowe, Associate Director (President of Hockey Operations, Edmonton Oilers)

Coaches

Mike Babcock, Head Coach (Coach, Detroit Red Wings)

Ken Hitchcock, Associate Coach (Coach, Columbus Blue Jackets)

Jacques Lemaire, Associate Coach (Coach, New Jersey Devils)

Lindy Ruff, Associate Coach (Coach, Buffalo Sabres)

Goaltenders

Martin Brodeur, 37 (New Jersey Devils)

Marc-André Fleury, 25 (Pittsburgh Penguins)

Roberto Luongo, 30 (Vancouver Canucks)

Defencemen
Dan Boyle, 33 (San Jose Sharks)
Drew Doughty, 20 (Los Angeles Kings)
Duncan Keith, 26 (Chicago Blackhawks)
Scott Niedermayer, 36 (Anaheim Ducks)
Chris Pronger, 35 (Philadelphia Flyers)
Brent Seabrook, 24 (Chicago Blackhawks)
Shea Weber, 24 (Nashville Predators)

Forwards
Patrice Bergeron, 24 (Boston Bruins)
Sidney Crosby, 22 (Pittsburgh Penguins)
Ryan Getzlaf, 24 (Anaheim Ducks)
Dany Heatley, 29 (San Jose Sharks)
Jarome Iginla, 32 (Calgary Flames)
Patrick Marleau, 30 (San Jose Sharks)
Brenden Morrow, 31 (Dallas Stars)
Rick Nash, 25 (Columbus Blue Jackets)
Corey Perry, 24 (Anaheim Ducks)
Mike Richards, 25 (Philadelphia Flyers)
Eric Staal, 25 (Carolina Hurricanes)
Joe Thornton, 30 (San Jose Sharks)
Jonathan Toews, 21 (Chicago Blackhawks)

Hockey Canada Personnel

Bob Nicholson, President
Johnny Misley, Executive Vice-President
Wayne Gretzky, Special Advisor
Brad Pascall, Senior Director, Men's National Teams
Scott Salmond, Director, Men's National Teams
Ben Cooper, Video Manager
Jim Thorne, Team Doctor
Pierre Gervais, Equipment Manager
Pat O'Neill, Equipment Manager
Mike Burnstein, Athletic Therapist
Jim Ramsay, Athletic Therapist
Kent Kobelka, Therapist
André Brin, Media Relations
J.J. Hebert, Media Relations
Mark Black, Coordinator, Men's National Teams

LEAVE NO DOUBT

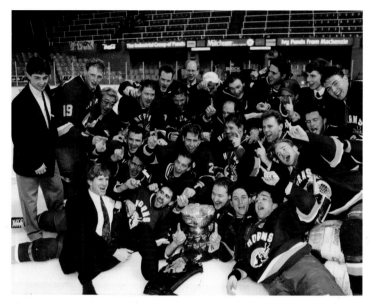

In 1994, the University of Lethbridge Pronghorns won their first and only national championship. It was a victory that saved the program. (Photo courtesy of Shelby MacLeod/University of Lethbridge Archives)

A big moment for some happy members of the Canadian junior team in 1997. They're singing the national anthem after winning gold at the World Junior Championships at Geneva. (Photo courtesy of Gerry Thomas)

In 2004, Canada won the World Championships in Prague.
Our slogan was "For Our Kids," and our gold medal triggered
a six-figure donation to youth hockey in Canada.
(Jiri Kolis/Hockey Hall of Fame)

A dream come true. The Red Wings beat Pittsburgh in the Stanley Cup finals in 2008. That's Nick Lidstrom, the team captain, holding the Cup. (Photo courtesy of Dave Reginek, Detroit Red Wings)

In 1997 we did it, and it was our dream that we would do it again at the Vancouver 2010 Olympics: have the chance to sing our national anthem.
(Photo courtesy of Jeff Vinnick/Hockey Canada)

Top: Drinking out of the Stanley Cup – no beer has ever tasted so good. (Photo courtesy of Dave Reginek, Detroit Red Wings)

Bottom: Scotty Bowman was used to winning the Stanley Cup – he's had his name etched on it 12 times. He was a special advisor to the Red Wings in 2008. My assistant coach Todd McLellan and I were thrilled to have our first. (Photo courtesy of Dave Reginek, Detroit Red Wings)

THE CREDO

Leave No Doubt

That this is our game.

That this is our time.

That 14 days in February will be two weeks for the ages.

That every day counts.

That every meeting matters.

That every practice makes a difference.

That each one of us will rise to every occasion.

That this isn't about us, it's about our country.

That we know 33 million Canadians will attend every game.

That home ice is an advantage.

That nothing can distract us.

That nothing will stop us.

That our determination will define us.

That we are built to win.

That we are a team of character.

That we are a team of destiny.

So let the world be warned on February 28, 2010 we will ...

LEAVE NO DOUBT

INTRODUCTION

This isn't just a book about hockey. It's about life.

While the story is anchored in Canada's 2010 gold medal-winning Olympic experience, it's really about potential, pressure, and turning dreams into reality. This book isn't a chronological, game-by-game review of the Olympics. It's a book of perspective; snapshots of moments. It's about learning moments – big and small.

Each chapter is headlined by a phrase from the "Leave No Doubt" credo that hung in our dressing room throughout the two weeks of the 2010 Vancouver games. While the credo was written specifically for the Olympics, it represents my approach to life, to competing, and to chasing dreams. It's an approach that I've embraced as an everyday commitment.

You'll find that each chapter ends with a question. As a lifelong learner – with a lot still left to learn – and someone who tries to surround himself with smart people, I've always liked questions. I think too many of us are too busy trying to prove we have the answers, and not enough of us are asking questions. The right question can unlock life-changing possibilities. Hopefully, some of mine do for you.

At the back of the book, I've included personal definitions of words such as integrity, gratitude, commitment, and potential. I think words mean different things to different people. I want you to know what they mean to me. A friend of mine says the words are part of "The Babcock Dictionary."

For me, they are words that make a difference.

I wrote this book because I want to help.

I want to help people who want to make moments happen. People who understand that days, months, and even years can blur, but moments make up the photo album of your memory. Moments happen when we meet our potential. Moments happen when we make a difference. Moments happen when dreams become reality. I want to help people who are willing to commit to their dreams.

There are a lot of ways to chase your dreams. I believe in chasing dreams with your eyes open.

Dreaming with your eyes open is about having a plan. It's about doing. It has nothing to do with wishful thinking, or in closing your eyes and hoping. Don't get me wrong, hope can be a great thing – but if you want to reach your potential, you need a well thought-out approach.

Chasing your dreams with your eyes open is anchored in the power of everyday commitment. Everyday commitment is the biggest gift you can give yourself. You have to earn your dreams. Everyday commitment gives you a shot at doing just that.

Being fully committed is full of challenge and joy.

What could be more fun than chasing your dreams with everything you have?

An everyday commitment to your dreams makes them real. I believe dreaming is one of the most powerful forces on the planet. Dreams can drive action, fuel change, and accomplish the impossible. I'm a hockey coach. That's what I do. But each and every one of us – no matter what we do – has the chance to get better.

It doesn't matter who you are, it doesn't matter what your interests or passions are: you always have a chance to inspire, to change things, to make things better.

Dreams can make a difference. I believe committing to your dreams can make you a difference-maker.

If you've picked up this book, my bet is that you believe this too.

CHAPTER 1

LEAVE NO DOUBT (PART ONE)

Sunday, February 28th, 2010. Vancouver, Canada.

It was Canada against the United States in the gold medal game for men's hockey on the final day of the Olympics. Our entire nation was watching. And with 24 seconds left in the third period, the Americans scored the tying goal. My daughter Taylor, who was in the stands, slumped into her seat, put her head into her hands and burst into tears. Her reaction was a very personal one, but what she felt captured the emotion of people across our country.

Ownership of our game, our dream, our destiny was going into overtime.

It was a moment.

I think moments are what life is all about.

Moments can put dreams to the test. They are when dreams can come true.

Moments are what you remember.

"Leave No Doubt" are three words that I believe help create moments.

Basically, the credo of Leave No Doubt is a call to action. It's an ambition.

It goes after the one thing that stands in the way of your dreams and your ability to make a difference: doubt. We all have the ability to make a difference and turn dreams into reality. The energy we need to commit, progress, and achieve exists inside of each of us.

Doubt is the biggest energy-taker there is. It eats away at our emotional core. It drains us of mental energy and physical energy. It demoralizes, distracts, and de-motivates.

Doubt can paralyze you. And have a lasting impact if you don't push through it.

It's true for kids. It's true for adults. It's true for all of us.

I took some kids wakesurfing last summer at my cottage in Emma Lake, Saskatchewan. You get a big group of kids in the boat, the sun is shining and the music is blasting – life is good.

Kids started surfing. As more kids got into it and got up and surfed, you could see doubt beginning to surface in others. And avoidance started to set in for some – they waited while others went ahead of them. They were looking for reasons not to go – "It's no big deal. We're running out of time. I'll do it next time." The truth is, next time is always harder. Don't ever fool yourself into believing anything different.

My perspective is that if you feel doubt, go first. Jump in and give it a go.

I'm not a gambler, but I love "going for it." That's true in everything I do. And there have been many times in my life when I came face-to-face with doubt, but ultimately I learned how to push past it. I've learned that putting yourself out there is a great way to learn and grow. The more you push yourself the more you grow. Whether I'm waterskiing at Emma Lake or hunting big game up in Alaska, I love pushing to the edge. I love risk. Not stupid risk, but calculated risk that makes you better. The kind of risk that gets you activated – functioning in a way that pushes you beyond the limits of where you are to the next level of where you want to be.

A lot of people say "coulda, woulda, shoulda." But they never do.

That's doubt getting in the way. That's doubt getting in the way of your dreams.

You're not going to achieve that perfect surf the first time out. And that's okay. Take pride in trying. And when you fall short, don't ever hesitate trying again. Most times, you'll feel great about pushing through and getting after it. Why does trying feel great?

It's because you've taken on and beaten your toughest opponent – doubt.

Everybody comes face-to-face with doubt.

If we don't push through doubt, if we don't make doubt momentary, it gets stronger. It hits at the essence of who we are, who we want to be.

Whatever your game, your goal, or your dream, you will face doubt. Whenever you try to be better, try your best, or try something new, you will face doubt. Doubt shows up every time you challenge yourself. Getting past doubt isn't a "one-and-done" thing.

People who dream with their eyes open have a "stick-to-it-ive-ness" that helps them dig in and get them beyond their doubt.

Turning dreams into reality takes effort. You have to go out and make dreams happen.

In 1993, about five years into my coaching career, I was fired by the Moose Jaw Warriors of the Western Hockey League. I got into a disagreement with management and they let me go. My wife Rene – we pronounce it "Reenie" – and I had a three-month-old baby, Allie. Coming home to tell Rene that I'd been fired was one of the toughest things I've ever had to do. We had no money and I had few prospects.

What I did have was doubt. It was a setback. And setbacks open the door to doubt.

After I got fired, my wife and I both started looking for teaching jobs. They were hard to come by. We thought we had a pretty good shot at landing something in Strasbourg, Saskatchewan, a town of about 750 people. We knew people in town. We knew they'd put in a good word for us. But nothing came of it. At the same time, I had been pursuing an opportunity with RLG International, a business consulting firm. They offered me a job. And I accepted.

Then, out of nowhere, another opportunity knocked.

Looking back, it was really my "last shot" coaching opportunity.

I got an offer to coach the men's hockey team at the University of Lethbridge. The coach at Lethbridge, Dave Adolph, left and went to the University of Saskatchewan.

A reference from Pete Anholt, a former teammate and a guy in the coaching fraternity, helped put the offer on the table. At the time, the Lethbridge Pronghorns had a nucleus of good young players, but they had never made the playoffs and the program was at risk of shutting down.

The consulting job offered a lot more money, greater stability, and a clearer career path.

Ultimately, I chose to take a risk.

I took the coaching position in Lethbridge. I had to push through doubt to do it, but I wanted to chase my dream of being a hockey coach. I made the choice to jump in and give it a go.

My one year in Lethbridge, we captured the Pronghorns' first-ever national championship. Winning the nationals was an unbelievable feeling for me. It wasn't like I hadn't been with some good teams before then, but I had never won the big game in the end.

After that, I accepted a job as head coach of the Spokane Chiefs of the Western Hockey League. I had a six-year run in Spokane. We won more playoff games than any other team during that six-year period, including two conference titles. And it was the Spokane job that gave me the opportunity to coach the Canadian team at the World Junior Championships, where we won gold. That opened the door to an American Hockey League job with the Cincinnati Mighty Ducks, a shared farm team between Anaheim and Detroit of the National Hockey League.

After two years in Cincinnati, I got the call to be head coach of the Anaheim Mighty Ducks of the NHL. In 2003, my first year in Anaheim, we went to the Stanley Cup finals where we lost in seven games to the New Jersey Devils. But during that playoff run, we swept the defending Stanley Cup champion Detroit Red Wings. The Red Wings ended up hiring me as their head coach in 2005. And that's where I still am today – head coach of the Detroit Red Wings.

I'm not sure that anybody would have looked at me in 1993, as I began my stint as the head coach of the University of Lethbridge, and figured me for a good bet to be the head coach of Canada's hockey team at the 2010 Olympics in Vancouver.

Then again, if you put yourself out there, if you take a risk and face your doubt, good things can start to happen.

I'm living proof of that.

Don't doubt your dreams.

The Leave No Doubt credo embodies my approach to making dreams happen.

It provides a way to get things done. It's a way to progress.

The credo evolved from my desire for us to have a unifying theme for the Olympics. Looking back at my other international experiences, I felt like a theme helped to focus and energize us as a team. I believed it would help. I wanted something hanging in the dressing room that "talked" to our players, our coaches, our management – and to me. Obviously there would be a lot of things to focus and energize us throughout the Olympics, but success is in the margins. That's why I try to cover it all.

Once I had the idea for a unifying theme, I reached out to people I knew in business and marketing to see what we could come up with. It's always smart to reach out to people with different areas of expertise and experience when you're looking for ideas and new ways of doing things. I ended up connecting with a longtime friend, an advertising guy, Rick Larsen. We started a process of exchanging thoughts and bouncing around different lines.

The process of getting to the theme itself was fun and energizing. We hit on the line "Leave No Doubt" in the middle of July 2009. I was out on my ski boat, as I am every morning in summer, with some guys on Emma Lake. It was around 6:30 a.m. and Rick called. He was in his office on the 21st floor of the Leo Burnett Building in Chicago. We started talking and once we hit on the line, I knew we had nailed it.

Leave No Doubt really "spoke" to me. It's what I had been looking for.

But as Rick and I continued to talk, I realized there was an opportunity for more. Our conversations helped me crystallize a belief system and an approach to dreams, potential, and success that I have been living my whole life. So we kept working at it, and by the end of July the credo was written. I wanted a powerful message in the dressing room. I wanted every line to stand on its own. I got what I wanted. In the end, I believe the credo had an impact. It played its role.

The credo is something I continue to live by.

It's what I know.

It's what I know works.

It's an everyday commitment.

No doubt.

You can't overestimate the power of day-to-day commitment. It pushes us to change and grow.

For me, everyday commitment isn't a "have to" thing, it's a "want to" thing.

It's all in your attitude and how you choose to look at it. If you see commitment as a burden, it's a weight you won't be able to carry. I see commitment as a gift that unlocks all that's good. It pushes us to get better. Burden or gift: the choice is ours to make.

Ultimately, I believe commitment is about respect.

It's about respecting yourself and your potential to contribute. It's about respecting your teammates and the game you play. It's about respecting your company, your colleagues, and the way you do business. It's about respecting your friends and the people you come into contact with. And most importantly, commitment is about respecting and loving your family.

Commitment is about respecting the life you lead.

It's about being there for your family, friends, colleagues, and your teammates. And it's about being there for your goals and dreams too. It's about being on task. And it's about grinding it out when everybody else has given in. Commitment is about showing up.

If you're not willing to commit, your dreams simply become wishful thinking.

Dreams need to be chased. That's a powerful truth. But the gift of commitment gets you activated. Being activated means being fully engaged and having fun. It's being all-in. And being all-in is a great feeling.

Chasing your dreams with everything you have is a lot of fun.

Are you ready to commit to your dreams?

CHAPTER 2

THIS IS OUR GAME

"Henderson has scored for Canada …"

Paul Henderson's goal in the last minute of the final game lifted Canada to victory in the 1972 Summit Series against the Soviet Union. He rescued our pride as a hockey power and became a national folk hero. I remember the excitement of that moment. Time seemed to stop as fans across the country watched from the edge of their seats. They sat in homes and offices. And in schools too.

I was a nine-year-old boy in Leaf Rapids, Manitoba. It was a newly built mining town in the northern part of the province.

We sat with Mr. Jefferies in our little school, watching a game for the ages and cheering Canada on to victory.

Thinking back, it reminds me that hockey has been an important part of our national psyche for a long time. When Henderson put the puck in the back of the net, you could probably hear the collective sigh of relief and the shouts of celebration that followed in every corner of our country. Leaf Rapids, Manitoba, included.

There's nothing like a wake-up call.

The Canada–Russia Summit Series in 1972 let us know the hockey world was coming after us. Our hockey supremacy was being challenged.

Against the backdrop of the Cold War, the Soviets challenged a team of our best players in a way we had never seen before. Although the Soviets had been successful in Olympic hockey, Canadians never believed other countries could compete against our best professional talent (at that time, NHL players were not eligible to take part in the Olympics). The series captured the imagination of Canadians. People were glued to their TV sets. The hockey world had never seen this kind of tension and drama.

The stakes had never seemed higher. That series reminded us that it's only our game when we win.

And we needed a goal in the final minute to do it.

Little did I know then that, almost forty years later, Canada's 2010 Olympic hockey team would have our own game for the ages.

And that I would play a part in it.

Hockey is Canada's game. Canadians believe it.

For Canadians, hockey is a passion. Really, it's closer to an obsession. The game brings us joy and exhilaration. It's a game that brings us together. It's a game we know. It's a game we love. But we all realize that for us, hockey has always been more than a game. We play it, watch it, talk about it, and argue over it with an unrivalled devotion. It's part of who we are.

It is part of our national identity.

Kids all over Canada grow up playing the game. In big cities, on small farms; in the Maritimes, on the Prairies, and in every other region; right across this country, kids play and they dream. Day and night, on streets, driveways, frozen ponds, and rinks around the country, they dream of scoring the game-winning goal.

I was like every one of those kids, dreaming of that moment:

Arms raised.

Fists pumping.

Smiling from ear to ear.

Mobbed by teammates.

The roar of the crowd.

A dream come true.

In the end, it's hard to claim ownership of the game of hockey, or any game, if you don't win.

Fair or not, winning is the one thing people will remember.

February 2010 was an opportunity for us to assert our hockey supremacy by winning Olympic gold. We would be on home ice. Many believed it was our destiny to win gold long before the first puck was dropped. I was born in the small town of Manitouwadge, in northern Ontario, and was proud to have earned the huge opportunity of being Canada's head coach. In addition to my hockey credentials, I had lived in Ontario, Quebec, Saskatchewan, Alberta, Manitoba, British Columbia, and the Northwest Territories, so I felt uniquely connected to Canada's many different regions.

I truly felt privileged to be a part of our Olympic team.

Many believed the Olympics in Vancouver would be a dream come true for the 2010 team.

But dreams don't simply come true. A lot of interesting things can happen between expectation and achievement – between dreaming and fulfilling your dreams.

The chase was on.

Being appointed head coach of the Olympic team was the beginning of an unforgettable journey. I would experience our national obsession like never before.

Over the past forty years hockey has gone global, and today our game is embraced and loved internationally. Countries around the world carry a passion for hockey that rivals our own. The talent being infused into the game grows every year. And there are a number of countries that can rightfully consider themselves hockey powers.

In 2010 the Russians, Swedes, Czechs, and Americans all had legitimate shots at winning the gold medal. There were a lot of great teams and players there, but that didn't matter. It never will. As Canadians, we will always believe that hockey gold is our birthright. The expectation of gold was absolute.

Still, it was worth remembering that forty years ago, we learned a birthright can't score a goal or stop a puck.

We had to be ready for the challenge.

We had to embrace the expectation.

We had to chase the nation's dream with our eyes open.

Whatever it is – your game, your goal, your dream – you have to "own it."

Individually or as a team, ownership is about having skin in the game and feeling responsible. Taking ownership raises the stakes. Things become more personal, more a reflection of who you are. As a result, you give more, you work harder and you learn faster. And that makes things happen. Owning your dreams fuels passion.

You can direct your passion towards good works, a business venture, or sports. It can keep an afterschool program alive, it can help provide for those less fortunate, it can comfort those in pain, it can help come up with a way to minimize our carbon footprint, or it can help you land your dream job.

Passion and taking ownership can do a lot of things.

Without them, you can't take a legitimate shot at anything.

When we got to Vancouver the atmosphere was electric.

I've never felt anything like it. There was so much energy, so much excitement, and so much anticipation. It was amazing.

2010 had all the pieces in place for two weeks in February to be a storybook moment.

There are moments in life where you are simply the right person, at the right place, at the right time. You have a chance to make a difference. And you feel something special is going to happen.

The 2010 Olympics was one of those moments for me. I felt in my heart and in my mind that we were going to get it done. On home ice, in front of our fans, we would do our part to help Canada "Own the Podium" – a credo that had been adopted by the Canadian Olympic Committee.

In Vancouver, you could feel the excitement and anticipation around "what could be." I think the Canadian people – athletes, volunteers, and spectators alike – outdid themselves at the Olympics. As Canadians, we reached out and embraced the world. And the world embraced us back. There was a lot of pride to be felt.

Pride in being Canada.

Pride in hosting the world.

Pride in being part of the global community.

And everybody was having a lot of fun.

It was a uniquely Canadian kind of pride – fun-loving, laidback, and welcoming. And it was contagious.

My oldest daughter Allie described it best when she said we were out there "generously spreading the spirit." It was just people being real: wanting to make friends, wanting to make a connection, and wanting to be part of something bigger. People wanted to create memories and moments that would last a lifetime. I can't think of a moment when I was more proud to be Canadian. People were feeling great about our country, wherever they were coming from. Everybody was having a great time.

I was inspired by it all.

The venues, the volunteers, the fans. I saw dreams come true. I saw dreams crushed. I saw hearts filled with joy. I saw hearts broken. I saw people embrace pressure and defy expectations. I saw people overcome doubt. I saw people do the impossible.

When Alex Bilodeau won gold in freestyle skiing to became the first Canadian ever to win gold on our home soil and stood at the bottom of Cypress Mountain hugging his brother – what a moment! Or when Tessa Virtue and Scott Moir became the first North American skaters, and the youngest competitors in the history of the sport, to win Olympic gold in ice dancing, it made the hair on the back of my neck stand up.

Through it all, the Olympic spirit was everywhere – the sportsmanship, the camaraderie, and the love of the game – whatever that game may have been. I came away from Vancouver with such respect for every single competitor at the Games. Each and every one of them competed with everything they had, whether they medaled or not.

Every one of them was driven by a passion. Every one of them committed. Every one of them had taken ownership of their dreams.

Have you taken ownership of your dreams?

CHAPTER 3

THIS IS OUR TIME

Before I left for Vancouver, we sat down as a family to talk about all of us going to the Olympics.

It was a once-in-a-lifetime thing. Rene and I sat down with our three kids – Allie, Michael, and Taylor – and spoke about doing it right. Allie and Michael would have to miss a couple weeks of high school and Taylor would have to miss a couple weeks of junior high, but they wanted to be there. And I wouldn't have had it any other way. We talked about being grateful for the chance we had been given. We talked about the fun we would have taking it all in – going to the venues, watching Canadian athletes compete against the best in the world, and together, just soaking in the Olympic experience as a family.

Experiencing the Olympics as a family was important to me. Sharing the ups, the downs, the joy and exhilaration would make the Olympics that much better.

Family always makes everything that much better.

We also sat down as a family and had another conversation. A conversation not a lot of other families had heading into the Olympics.

We had the "what if" conversation.

As coach of Canada's hockey team I was well aware of the expectations for Olympic gold.

I was also aware of the pressure my family would feel during the games. Brian Burke, the general manager of Team USA, said "The pressure started for Team Canada the day they awarded the games to Vancouver." He was right. My kids felt some of that pressure. They wanted the team and *their* Dad to bring home the gold for our country.

I told the kids we would do our best; that I would do my best. Basically, I asked of myself what I have always asked of them. The conversation was for them, but it was also for me. If we didn't come home with the gold medal, someone would be held accountable. The head coach would be a natural place to start. We talked about the size of the opportunity and what was at stake. Talking about the "what if" helped me put things in perspective.

I told them I felt confident we were going to get it done.

But I also acknowledged the chance that it wouldn't work out.

Rene and I are doing our best to raise our kids to be difference-makers. We encourage them to put themselves out there, do their best, maximize their potential. Going out to Vancouver was an opportunity for me to put myself out there and do my best, for me to go out and maximize my potential.

It's an interesting thing when you put yourself out there and get to a big moment. My kids have watched their Dad lose twice in Game Seven of the Stanley Cup finals. In 2003, they flew back to Anaheim after a Game Seven loss in New Jersey. In 2009, they drove back home from Joe Louis Arena in Detroit after a Game Seven loss to Pittsburgh. Those were two long trips home.

Losing when you're that close is tough. It rips your heart out – momentarily. But what's done is done. Two days later, you're proud for having got as far as you did. You have to get there. You have to win 15 games in the playoffs to have the ultimate shot at the greatest trophy in the sports world – Lord Stanley's Cup.

You also pause at those kinds of moments, when winning or losing puts a lot on the line. You stop and think about what's really important.

Ultimately, I believe the measure of a man isn't taken in gold medals, Stanley Cups, awards, promotions, raises, or material accomplishments of any kind. I believe you're measured by the family you raise. Are they good people? Do they have integrity? Do they embrace the importance of giving back? In the end, that's what really matters.

I always tell my kids that there's no such thing as peer pressure. I tell them that doing the right thing is cool. I think people are attracted to that. It shows confidence, strength, and backbone. Doing right, doing the very best you can, is what makes you who you are. I believe results are important, and winning is great, but in the end it's not what defines who you are.

However, that kind of perspective is easy to lose.

It never hurts to remind yourself of what's really important.

Whether we won gold or not, I was going to be the same man. My family wouldn't change. I was going to Vancouver as a proud Olympian, to experience an Olympic Games in a way few people get a chance to. I wanted to be at my best for my country and my team. Absolutely. And I was determined to have the experience, whatever the outcome, make me a better coach and a better person.

The Olympics would be one of those defining moment opportunities. But whether we won or lost, it wasn't going to be the measure of who I am.

You have to embrace opportunities for all they are worth. That's how you create memories. And for me, that's what life is all about – creating memories.

Vancouver would be unforgettable.

— · — · —

It's exciting to get yourself into position to do something special. You can't assume your time will come and things will simply fall into place for you. I believe you have to work your way into position. And it doesn't happen overnight. At least it didn't for me.

My career path has been a step-by-step journey. Every job I've had has been my dream job. It might sound like a stretch, but it's true. I never started out dreaming of being the coach of Canada's Olympic hockey team. My perspective is "Dream about the next job, dream about progressing, of getting better." I dreamt with my eyes open. I went at it one step at a time. I worked hard and earned my way. And, above all, I had a lot of fun doing it. Every coaching job I've taken has had its share of challenges, some jobs more than their fair share. You've just got to go all in and embrace what's in front of you. You've got to enjoy the process.

For me, it's been a journey that's been filled with great people, great opportunities, great experiences, and lots of momentary setbacks. I've been lucky. I've followed my passion and it's pushed me to pursue excellence. A lot of being successful is being in the right place at the right time. And recognizing, when it's your time, you have to take your shot. But I'm also a big believer in having a success-oriented mindset.

In my yearbook from Holy Cross High School in Saskatoon, I answered the question "What do you want to be?" by saying: "My ambition, like many of yours, is to succeed in whatever I do." I didn't really know what "succeed" meant for me at the time, but I still believed it.

If I'm really honest about it, I have to thank my Mom for first kicking me into gear. Back in 1987, I was player-coach of a semi-pro team in Whitley Bay, England. I was having a lot of fun and getting pretty good at not taking anything too seriously. In the summer when I got back to Saskatoon, my Mom looked me in the eye and said: "You know, Michael, at some point your beer-commercial lifestyle is going to have to come to an end."

That was my Mom. Her description was pretty much on the money. She always had a great way to tell me just what I needed to hear.

We all need people like that in our life.

Not too long after that, my brother-in-law, Doug Schwandt, told me about a job opening for the hockey coach of Red Deer College. At the time, I thought interviewing in Red Deer would be a great way to get me to the Calgary Stampede – one of the biggest parties in Canada. It wasn't the highest-order motivation, but a trip to Red Deer took me most of the way to Calgary. So I drove up to Red Deer, got to the college, changed into my suit in the parking lot at the school across the street, ran into the interview, sat before their board, and answered questions about why I should be the next head coach. I didn't have a lot of experience and I'm not sure I was qualified, but I believed I could do the job. And in the end I got the offer. One man, Al Ferchuk, saw something in me and gave me a chance. To this day, I'm grateful to Al and the board for giving me that first opportunity.

You just never know when your moment will come.

Sometimes all you need is a chance. Reach out and grab it when it comes. I mean, if you're going to go after something, you might as well go hard, right?

When I got the offer from Red Deer, my first reaction was "Oh my God, can I really do this?"

The doubt I felt was real but brief. I didn't dwell on the things I didn't know or the experience I didn't have. I pushed past my doubt by focusing on the task at hand. At some point, you really just have to go for it. It's as scary and simple as that. You have to do what you do and learn as you go. If you hesitate, if you wait for the timing or situation to be absolutely right, you'll spend your entire life in the waiting room.

I felt like I had landed my dream job.

I've had six dream jobs since that one in Red Deer, including my job as coach of the Detroit Red Wings. That's just the way I feel about it. And with every opportunity, I've had a moment of doubt, an "Oh my God, can I really do this job?" reaction. And every time the doubt was just that – momentary. I pushed past my doubt every time. Focus and commitment always helped me do it.

So did success. Every small success I achieved helped me get beyond doubt a little faster the next time.

Belief in yourself helps too.

It's not about being cocky or arrogant. It's about a deep belief and confidence in what you're capable of doing.

Everybody hopes for success.

That's okay, but you can't just hope your way to success. Difference-makers get on task and start doing. And it's funny, the harder I've worked, the luckier I've gotten. I bet that's true for most of us. And I believe that part of being lucky is feeling lucky. Feeling fortunate. Blessed.

Attitude makes a difference. And you have the power to choose your attitude every day.

Here's something given to me by Scotty Bowman. He told me he carries it in his wallet. It's from "Attitude" by Charles Swindoll.

"The longer I live, the more I realize the impact of attitude on life. Attitude to me is more important than facts. It is more important than the past, than education, than money, than circumstances, than failures, than successes, than what other people think or say or do. It is more important than appearance, giftedness or skill. It will make or break a company ... a church ... a home. The remarkable thing is that we have a choice every day regarding the attitude we will embrace for that day. We cannot change our past ... we cannot change the inevitable. The only thing we can do is play on the one string we have, and that is our attitude ... I am convinced that life is 10% what happens to me and 90% how I react to it. And so it is with you ... we are in charge of our Attitudes."

I've got this quote pinned to the wall behind my desk. I've always believed in the power of attitude.

The Olympics were no different.

February 2010 would be our time.

Do you believe your time has come?

CHAPTER 4

TWO WEEKS FOR THE AGES

Difference-makers believe that if you can dream it, you can do it.

When I was named head coach of the Olympic hockey team, the sense of responsibility hit me hard. This wasn't about me, this was about our game. This was about our country, about our national pride. And this was about having a chance to win the Olympic gold medal – on Canadian soil.

Two weeks in February would be a defining time. Two weeks full of meaningful moments.

It was two weeks that would make a lifelong difference to the players, coaches, and management of Team Canada. And it was two weeks that would make a difference to Canadians.

One way or another it would give us something to remember.

It would be something people would talk about, discuss, and debate for years to come.

You just knew it.

My youngest daughter, Taylor, had an interesting take on things. I got the Olympic head coaching job in June 2009. After we lost Game Seven of the Stanley Cup finals to Pittsburgh on a Friday, we gathered for a team picture the following Monday. Steve Yzerman asked me to stop by his office where he told me, "Mike, you're going to be the coach of the Canadian Olympic team."

I thanked him for the opportunity. What a dream come true! When I got to my truck, I called my wife immediately to share the great news. When I got home and told my kids, Taylor said: "Dad, the reason you lost in Game Seven was because you can't win everything. And you're going to win at the Olympics."

Clearly, the pressure was on.

I didn't realize it, but I had been preparing for the Olympic moment my whole life.

From my first head coaching job at Red Deer College, through my years coaching in juniors and in the minors, to seven years as a head coach in the NHL including three Stanley Cup finals, as well as my international experience, I was confident and battle-tested. I was ready to be Canada's coach.

But first and foremost, I felt like I was prepared because of the values instilled in me by my parents. I was given a great foundation by my Mom and Dad. One of my lasting memories as a kid was driving with my Dad to the open pit at the Leaf Rapids mine in Manitoba. Dad managed the mine. One day I asked, "Dad, how do you get the people here to work hard for you?" I've always remembered his answer. He said, "Son, you can never ask anybody to work harder than you work yourself." I learned about work from my Dad.

I love that. I live that.

I drive people hard, but no harder than I drive myself. Leadership is about modeling. It's as much about what you do as what you say. You set a tone. Yes, I'm demanding but I'm also supportive. I'm respectful. If I make a mistake I acknowledge it, correct it and move on. I'm about continual improvement. I work hard, really hard. My coaches and I put everything we had into preparing for the Olympics. And the players were prepared to leave everything they had on the ice.

Olympic opportunities don't come along very often.

We would make the most of it.

As Canada's head coach I wanted my family and friends to be proud.

I wanted the people of Canada to be proud.

Back in 2002, when I was coaching the Detroit/Anaheim farm team in Cincinnati, the Olympics were in Salt Lake City and Canada was playing the United States in the gold medal game. Rene and I hosted a party that started with a cross cul-de-sac road hockey game. My kids were wearing Canadian jerseys, the other kids were in USA jerseys. We battled right there for hockey supremacy. And then we all went in to watch the game and Canada's gold-medal victory. It was a great neighborhood party. Everybody had a blast.

In 2010, I wanted every Canadian, in every little town, every big city, and every farm across our country, to have the chance to play, party, and celebrate our hockey supremacy. I wanted them to feel that hockey was our game and that nobody could take it away from us. I wanted them to feel like this was our moment and that nothing could keep us from it.

And finally, I wanted my Mom, who has always been a great source of inspiration and someone I never wanted to let down, to look on from Heaven and smile at what we were about to get done.

Cancer took her at the age of 51, only a few short years after she reminded me about my beer-commercial lifestyle in England. I was 28 when she passed away. I had a special bond with my Mom. She was a great lady. She was smart and strong. Growing up, all my high-school friends would love coming over just to talk with her. They'd be in the house half an hour before I even knew they were there. She was a great listener. And she made people feel good because of it. She believed in maximizing what you had been given. She believed in being a difference-maker. She believed in enjoying life, and felt the best way to enjoy things was by being all-in.

My Mom encouraged me to go after things with everything I had.

Whatever the outcome, I promised myself, my Mom was going to be proud of our Olympic effort.

I knew that Canada had never won hockey gold on home ice.

As recently as the 2006 Olympics, we hadn't even made it to the medal round. I knew our history in Olympic hockey had shown the task would be tough – we had only won gold twice in the last sixty years, in 1952 and 2002. I knew there were going to be a lot of talented teams at the games. I knew the Russians, Swedes, Czechs, and Americans were coming in loaded.

The Russians were super talented and had won the two previous world championships. The Swedes were a great team and played with no ego. They'd "out-patience" you and wait for you to make a mistake. They won the Olympic gold in 2006. The Czechs were as talented as the Russians. And the USA came in with Ryan Miller, the best goalie in the NHL at the time.

Many of the players I coached in Detroit would be taking the ice in Vancouver as our opponents. And they would be tough opponents. For me, this just added to the excitement. To be the best, you have to beat the best. It would be a privilege to line up opposite Nick Lidstrom, Pavel Datsyuk, Henrik Zetterberg, Brian Rafalski, Johan Franzen, Nick Kronwall, or Val Filppula as they represented their countries. I had so much respect for each and every one of them and their national teams that I'd be cheering for them every time they weren't playing against us. The talent on the ice at any one time was going to be phenomenal.

It was going to be something to see.

Flying over to Vancouver, I couldn't help but feel a kind of Olympic energy building inside of me.

I thought back to a memory of my son Michael in 2004. We had missed the playoffs with Anaheim, and I was working as an analyst for TSN. I was covering the Toronto–Ottawa series, and Pat Quinn and Jacques Martin were the respective coaches. After the morning skate, Michael, who was nine years old at the time, said, "Dad, let's go down and meet some NHL coaches." And I responded, "You know, son, your dad's an NHL coach." To which Michael replied: "Yeah Dad, but they're *good* ones. They've coached at the Olympics!" Both Quinn and Martin were on the Canadian coaching staff in Salt Lake City in 2002.

My Olympic opportunity had arrived. We were bringing our best, and the best would be expected from us. It was exhilarating. If I hadn't been wearing a seatbelt, I might have been pacing the entire flight. But then I did what I always do. I calmed down, cleared my head, and got down to work.

Another thing my Dad taught me was to stay calm under pressure. People often say to me that there's never a reaction from me, no matter what's going on. That's my Dad's advice kicking in. When you're under pressure and something goes wrong, stay calm. When a problem comes up, stay calm. Sure, there's a reaction inside. But on the outside, when it matters, I'm as calm as it gets. I believe that's what leaders do – stay calm, stay clear-headed, stay focused.

It's something that becomes more valuable the more pressure you're under.

The flight was an opportunity for me to dig in and work out some details on our Olympic day-to-day process. The more pressure you're under, the more you have to rely on what got you there. Structure and foundation were key. Always remember the fundamentals. Always be prepared. It had been six months since we'd been together as a team. We needed to hit the ground running.

When we touched down, the thing that hit you was the overwhelming energy of the people. As soon as I walked off the plane, I got the "I've got to deliver" feeling big time. I was ready to go. Our management team and support staff had done a great job every step of the way getting us ready for day one in Vancouver.

Now, as coaches, it was our turn.

A key step in hitting the ground running was the development of our team structure and the foundation we had built at our players' camp the previous summer. So when we first stepped on the ice to practice, it was like turning on a light bulb again. It lit up a familiarity with what we were doing.

It set us right from the beginning of our journey.

Our opening game was against Norway. We had our 10 o'clock team meeting the night before – just like we would every night before a game during the Olympics.

You could feel the emotion in the room. I tried to take a step back and just, for a second, take it all in. It was so exciting, and a lot of fun being a part of it all. I was surrounded by people of talent and character. People with passion. People who knew how to get the job done. People united in achieving one goal.

There was nowhere else I would have rather been.

I didn't give an emotional speech that night. Why get the players even more revved up before they have to go to bed? There was more than enough emotion in the room. The moment sent the message. We all knew why we were here and what our job was.

As the hockey competition started you could feel the anticipation and expectations hitting a fever pitch all around us. Norway was not going to be a big test for us, but there wasn't a team in the tournament that was going to roll over.

Reputation means nothing once the puck is dropped.

Do you look at life as moments of opportunity?

CHAPTER 5

EVERY DAY COUNTS

Tuesday, February 16th, 2010.

It was time to drop the puck and do what we do.

The roar of the sold-out crowd was deafening. This was Game One for the 2010 Olympic team. You could almost feel the level of expectation taking the roof off Canada Hockey Place.

I think some media people figured we should score every time we touched the puck against Norway.

I knew that given the buildup, nothing could satisfy expectations out of the gate. And I knew every move, line change and tactic would be put under a microscope. We beat Norway 8–0. We dominated play and outshot them 42–15. For many, it wasn't enough.

You can't worry about the expectations of others. Or what other people might do. There's a saying I like to use as a reminder: "If you listen to what the media or the fans expect or want you to do, pretty soon you'll be sitting with them."

You have to do what you think is right. That's why you're standing behind the bench.

There were some big decisions coming.

Game One was done.

Our journey had begun.

Preparation is a step-by-step thing. Winning is a step-by-step thing. Success is a step-by-step thing.

I know it doesn't seem very exciting or revolutionary. That's because it isn't – but it *is* effective.

Having a process helps you make things happen.

I believe in a process, an approach, a way of living that's built around getting progressively better. I believe in day-to-day. I believe in the power of digging in and grinding it out. I believe in taking care of the details. It's what real pros do.

Make process your partner. It'll help you stay on task. It'll accelerate your progress.

Every day is a chance to get better. Every day you have a chance to deliver. That's where the excitement, joy, and fun are.

You have to enjoy the grind, or you'll burn yourself out before you reach your goal. And you have to embrace and celebrate each day for the progress you make. If you don't feel like you've made progress, celebrate your effort. Success is a marathon, not a sprint.

And endurance needs joy.

I think about some of the great Red Wings of all time. Take Gordie Howe. For all his talent, physical capabilities, and mental toughness, he was a force to be reckoned with into his fifties because of the joy he got from the game. Mr. Hockey, as Howe is known, is an amazing man. If he taught us anything, it's that pushing toward your dreams should be a labor of love. The same could be said for other great hockey players, like Ted Lindsay, Alex Delvecchio, Steve Yzerman, and Nick Lidstrom; it's true too for great hockey men such as Scotty Bowman, Ken Holland, Jimmy Devellano, and Jimmy Nill. Passion oozes out of these guys. They love the game. They love it all.

Every member of Team Canada had that same kind of passion. Each and every one of them had a passion and love for the game that you had to admire. Beyond their world-class talent, every player, coach and member of management had a desire to excel that was contagious. It created an atmosphere that was unbelievable to be a part of.

Significant achievement is built on small things, being all-in until it's all done, and loving what you do.

Loving what you do is a great way to make every day count.

I call the core of my step-by-step approach the "Circle of Success." It's anchored in everyday commitment.

A key part of the fabric that ties the Circle of Success together is an appreciation of the details.

Do you know why Nick Lidstrom is one of the greatest to ever play the game? First is his immense talent. But another thing about Nick is he never gets bored with the details. He embraces doing the same simple things over and over again. He takes great care in every detail and understands that repetition is the key to preparation, process, and performance. The guy tapes his stick today with the same meticulous pride and attention that he did as a rookie. It's amazing, really. He knows it all counts.

Here's my Circle of Success process – preparation drives execution, execution leads to success, success gets reinforcement, reinforcement grows confidence, confidence raises expectations, expectations drive excellence, and excellence demands greater preparation.

It's a virtuous circle that never stops.

In other words, the better prepared you are, the better you perform. The better you perform, the more you're rewarded. The more rewarded you are, the more confident you get. The more confident you get, the more you expect. The more you expect, the harder the drive to improve. The harder you drive, the more you prepare.

Bottom line, it's a process aimed at driving to progressive success and making continual improvement to help you deliver in big moments.

Our Olympic captain was Scott Niedermayer. I've known Scott for a long time. I coached him in the 2004 World Championships and competed against him. He's an amazing competitor and leader. And no matter how good he was, he always seemed to get better in the big moments. Too often I was on the wrong side of his talent. As far back as the playoffs in 2003, when he was playing for the New Jersey Devils, we called him "the ghost" because he did things on the ice that human beings just shouldn't be able to do.

In the 2007 playoffs, I was coaching the Red Wings versus Scott's Anaheim Ducks. He made a great play in Game Five to tie the game 1–1 and set them up for an overtime win. We went to Anaheim for Game Six and they knocked us out of the playoffs. Then they went on to beat Ottawa for the Stanley Cup. I believe if Scott doesn't make that play in Game Five, we win the Cup. Those kinds of plays and his quiet, confident leadership were the reasons why he was our captain at the Olympics.

In the end, it's all about learning. Learning to be your best and perform at your best when it matters most. In my experience, superstars tend to be "super-learners." In their own way, they have all mastered the Circle of Success. It's how difference-makers do what they do.

It's a hockey thing. It's a sports thing.

It's also a life thing.

At the Olympics, we had fourteen days. Fourteen days to come together. Fourteen days to execute on the Circle of Success.

I knew there were going to be ups and downs. I knew we'd face adversity. Adversity can challenge confidence and can open the door to doubt. The tough thing about adversity is that you don't know where or when it's going to show up. Or what it's going to look like when it does, or how long it's going to last. It could be an injury, a mistake, or a misunderstanding. It could be a negative opinion or criticism. Or an unexpected set of circumstances.

I believe adversity is a springboard to future success. It can make you better. It can make you stronger. I believe it works that way in hockey. I believe it works that way in business. I believe it works that way in education. I believe it works that way in life.

An every day, step-by-step approach is key to turning adversity into a springboard.

Teams that are prepared and focused, teams that are disciplined make adversity work *for* them. Not against them. We were that kind of team.

If you're going to progress, if you're going to excel, you're going to face adversity. Nobody really wants to face adversity. But if you live your life letting adversity get the best of you, you'll get nowhere. You can't close your eyes and wish adversity away.

You've got to embrace being put to the test.

Too often people think of tests as something bad, something to avoid or fear. But try thinking about tests as ways to accelerate progress, as challenges that can get us "further, faster" in our pursuits.

Adversity can change the trajectory of our careers, our contributions, and even our lives.

The Olympics would prove to be the ultimate test.

Our second game was against Switzerland.

A lot of people thought it would be an easy one for us, but I knew the Swiss would be tough. They played an NHL style. They beat Canada at the Turin Olympics in 2006 and I knew it hadn't been a fluke. This would be our first real test.

The Swiss played aggressively. And with a lot of confidence.

The game went to a shoot-out. After the first shoot-out round of three shots each, the game was still tied. So it went to a second round, and the same players could be called on again.

I called on Sidney Crosby one more time. And Sid won it for us with our first shot in the second round. A lot of people thought I chose him a second time simply because he was Sidney Crosby. The fact is, he got a second chance because, statistically, he was the best in the NHL in shoot-out goal percentage. We had done our homework and it paid off. Sid came through.

The final score was 3–2. The Swiss had carried the play at points in the game. We had some work left to do.

Still, it was a great win for us.

I knew it wasn't getting anything but tougher from here on in. Teams would be coming at us hard. They all wanted to be the team to knock off Team Canada.

We had a big bull's eye on our back.

The gold medal would not be given to us. We'd have to take it.

Do you make adversity work for you?

CHAPTER 6

EVERY MEETING MATTERS

You shouldn't have a meeting if it's not going to matter.

Meetings need to provide an action plan. If they don't, they're a waste of time.

I have a rule I learned from Scotty Bowman. I don't talk to players after a game. I shake their hands when we win and I leave them alone when we lose. You want to say the right thing, at the right time, for the right impact. In my experience, talking to players after a loss isn't usually the right time. Things are said in the heat of a moment that can be counter-productive or wrong.

Things can also be taken the wrong way. It's tough to pull words back once they are out of your mouth.

If you're still mad or disappointed in the morning, you probably have a reason to be. The morning gives you perspective. It gives you clarity. Perspective helps you address things in the right way. One of the smartest things you can do as a leader is give yourself some time to get into the right mindset for a meeting.

The toughest meetings are when there's an issue to be addressed.

People don't ask for feedback because they're afraid of what they might hear. But feedback is a very effective way to accelerate learning and performance – as long as it's constructive and clear. For some tough meetings, I will invite a player over to my house. Sometimes it's good to take a meeting out of your office and into a more relaxed place. As a leader, you know that time and place are key to getting across your message.

It can make it easier to talk like "people," instead of player and coach.

In Game Three we lost to the United States.

The game was high-tempo and very physical. Brian Rafalski, a defenceman who played for me in Detroit, scored two goals and added an assist for the Americans. For us, it was a tough loss.

After the game, in the dressing room, I broke my rule: I did talk to the players. But I waited. I let the players shower and change before I spoke to them. I gave the emotion a chance to settle. This was a meeting that mattered.

I wasn't mad, but I was disappointed. So were our players.

We knew this loss – in front of the largest TV audience in Canadian history – would rattle the country. And that the players would have to deal with it. I met with the coaches and then Steve Yzerman before talking to the team. I wanted to make sure we were on the same page. It was important to get our message right. I wanted the players to know what I thought. I wanted the players to know we played well. I told the boys that we outplayed the Americans. We did. We outshot them 45–23 and carried the play for most of the game.

Did we make mistakes? Yeah. I told them not to make more of it than it was. We lost. It was over. Would we get better? Sure, we would. You can get hung up on the negative. Losing to the Americans meant we would have to play an extra game to qualify for the quarter-finals. We would use the game we gained to get better.

This was one of those moments where it's important for coaches to remember they're not coaching players, they're coaching people.

At the beginning of the Games, Steve Yzerman held a meeting with the families of all the players. He talked about our Olympic opportunity, and what it meant to be a team. He said that every player on the Olympic team was a superstar on their own NHL team. They played on the power play. They played on the penalty kill. They played in the first minute. They played in the last minute. They were the go-to guys. And he reminded the families that on this team, it might be different. All the players would be treated fairly, but they might need their families' help in adjusting to a smaller role.

He talked about being committed to a common goal, and how every player would be asked to do whatever it took to help us succeed. He also talked about the importance of staying positive and the role family members played in this.

The families had to embrace the huge role they could play in relieving the pressure the players were under.

Steve had done his homework in advance.

And the role of the families was never more important than after the loss to the Americans.

After the game, we encouraged the team to go out and enjoy their families. We'd get back to the rink the next day and get better. We'd make the most of our chance to play an extra game. We wanted to convey a positive, calm demeanor. As I've said, leadership is about modeling, and as coaches we wanted to define the team's perspective coming off the loss. We wanted them to see and feel our confidence: to feel our confidence in them as a team.

We wanted to get the players' mindset right before we left the rink. Any doubts we had would be put in their proper place. They would be momentary, and we would move forward.

Ultimately, adversity would help us better prepare. It would help us win.

Having to play Germany in Game Four would help us get ready for Russia in the quarter-final.

When teams are operating under big pressure, you have to narrow their focus.

It's easy to unnerve them. It's easy to overwhelm them. It's easy to lose focus. We had to focus on the task at hand. Players had to concentrate on their roles and responsibilities.

We didn't want any distractions entering the dressing room after the loss. We didn't want any doubt coming into the equation. We didn't want any outside opinions telling our team what to think or how to react. We knew what to think and how to react. We knew what to do.

Conventional wisdom says that by losing to the United States, we made it more difficult for ourselves.

I don't agree with that. True, we had to play more games to get the gold. But the truth is, we needed to play more games to hit our stride and find our rhythm as a team.

We told the players that the loss to the US would give us one more game. One more game to get our lines set, one more game to get our system humming. It gave us, both coaches and players, time to break down our game, make adjustments and get our structure right.

Preparation never stops. It evolves game by game, opponent to opponent.

When you're under pressure, preparation is especially critical to performance because it fosters a sense of confidence. Preparation provides a sense of control, of being in charge of where you're going. Being underprepared is one way both individuals and teams allow for doubt to enter the frame.

Bottom line, productive meetings need three things.

One is rigorous preparation. Two is clarity of purpose. And three is an agreed-to action plan.

Anchoring your team in a clear mindset is a big part of preparation when you're under pressure. Ambiguity and confusion encourage doubt. Clarity minimizes it.

No one left our dressing room after the loss to the Americans with any doubt. The meeting helped us re-focus and get back on task. We were ready to move on.

Our goal was to win gold. That had not changed. It was a good time to face some adversity.

Do you make your meetings matter?

CHAPTER 7

IT'S ABOUT OUR COUNTRY

Some dreams are bigger than any one person.

2010 Olympic gold in hockey was our country's dream. The Swedes had won the gold in 2006. The Russians had won back-to-back world championships. The time was right to re-establish Canada's hockey supremacy.

We knew from the very beginning we had what it took to make the dream a reality.

Steve Yzerman set the tone the first night at the summer camp in 2009. He made it clear it wasn't about any one of us. He told the players, "I'm the general manager. Ken Holland, Kevin Lowe, and Doug Armstrong are all more experienced than me. Mike's the head coach. Jacques Lemaire, Lindy Ruff, and Ken Hitchcock are all more experienced than Mike. And they are willing to be called assistants. If these gentlemen didn't let ego get in the way, then you certainly will not."

To me, leadership is about serving your team's best interests. We came to Vancouver believing that we had chosen 23 leaders to play for Team Canada.

And at every opportunity they proved us right.

Depending on the moment, everybody on a team has a chance to lead in their own way.

As we approached our game with Germany, our goaltender Martin Brodeur was confronted with a big moment.

Martin Brodeur is one of the best goaltenders in the history of hockey. He had proven himself in the NHL and in international competition – winning Stanley Cups and an Olympic gold medal in 2002. He had a history of delivering when it counted.

After the loss to the USA with Brodeur in goal, we decided to start Roberto Luongo of the Vancouver Canucks in the next game against Germany. The tough thing with any great player is they always believe they can get the job done. Always. It's part of what makes them great. It's the part of them that makes them different. The great ones are a different kind of competitor. In 2008 in Detroit, we made the decision to replace Hall-of-Famer Dominik Hasek with Chris Osgood during our playoff run to the Stanley Cup. That's how this goaltending change would be measured. It was a tough decision to make, but it was a necessary decision. And we won, so it was the right decision. It was Lou's time. Vancouver was his city. He made the most of his opportunity.

I learned a couple of things from the Hasek situation. Get to the point and don't over-explain it. The players aren't interested in explanations: at least not in the moment. And that's the way I handled it with Brodeur.

I also knew that Steve Yzerman appointed me coach with these kinds of situations in mind. Steve knew me. He knew my experience. I wasn't going to be influenced by the fans, the media or the weight of the nation. I was simply going to be decisive. He expected and knew that I would do the right thing. Because of our relationship – I had coached Steve in 2005–2006, his final year as a player in Detroit, and had worked with him in the Red Wings organization since – he knew what he was going to get.

I went to Brodeur and told him that we'd be starting Lou against Germany. He said "Yup." That was it. Hard as it was, he took it like the pro he is. Through the rest of the games, Brodeur was nothing but supportive and positive.

Talk about leaving your ego at the door.

Martin Brodeur was proof that this team of superstars would do whatever it took to win for their country.

Leadership is probably the most talked-about, most written-about, most studied concept in all of sports and business. It's amazing how one genuine act of leadership can say so much.

It was a great leadership moment.

Remember, if we lose to Germany, the tournament is over for Canada and we leave the Olympics without a medal.

That wasn't going to happen. We ended up beating the Germans 8–2.

And for Team Canada, the Olympic Games were about to kick into high gear.

How is ego working for you, your team, your company?

CHAPTER 8

RISING TO EVERY OCCASION

Since 1972 Canada versus Russia has been the most intense rivalry in hockey.

The anticipation leading up to our game with Russia was incredible. You could feel it in the air. It was as if the anticipation from every part of the country had travelled to Vancouver and was sitting in the seats at Canada Hockey Place.

This would be a game remembered by hockey fans for generations to come. Many had expected these two teams to meet for the gold medal. Many now felt the winner would go on and take the gold. One thing was for certain, the loser would be going home with nothing: an inconceivable disappointment for both teams.

The game was one for the ages. It's hard to believe, but the last time Canada had beaten Russia (or the Soviet Union) in men's hockey at the Olympics was in Squaw Valley in 1960.

Still, that was ancient history. We were confident going in.

The final score was 7–3. Canada.

Some have said it's the best game ever played by a Canadian Olympic hockey team. We came out on fire. I mean absolutely on fire. And the noise from the stands was deafening. The players couldn't even hear us calling their names on the bench for the first three or four shifts. It was unbelievable. After the game, Russian goalie Ilya Bryzgalov said, "They came out like gorillas coming out of a cage. It was the most dominant big game I ever saw." I don't know about that, but we rose to the occasion.

It was sixty minutes of world-class hockey. No doubt.

We shut down their biggest threat: Alexander Ovechkin. We played him "five on one" with Jonathan Toews, Rick Nash, Mike Richards, Shea Weber, and Scott Niedermayer. Toews, Nash, and Richards really showed a lot of leadership. These guys are top-flight offensive superstars in the NHL. In fact Toews was our leading scorer in the Olympic tournament. After our loss to the Americans, we adjusted their roles. They became the match-up line. They were looking after the defensive side of the puck first. They weren't getting any power-play time.

They did what they did to help the team be better. They didn't give off any attitude or ask "Why us, why not them?" All they did was lead.

And deliver.

If you could ask Ovechkin, I'm sure he'd tell you.

As a team, we dominated the Russians in every aspect of the game. Each and every player did their little part and we were great together because of it.

Our loss to the USA helped us dominate Russia.

Dealing with adversity and coming up big can look different, depending on the situation.

In the end, rising to the occasion, whether on the ice, in an office or a classroom, means giving the world our very best. Meeting a moment head-on can be magic. Bringing everything you've got to a challenge – physically, mentally, and emotionally – is what defines the outcome. Facing adversity along the way can help you get where you want to go.

Working through adversity gives you confidence. Every time. And sometimes, working through adversity can inspire everyone around you.

Probably one of the most inspiring people I've ever met is Earl Cook.

I met Earl back in 2008. He was 20 years old. When I met him he had cancer and had lost a leg up to the hip to the disease. The cancer kept spreading. Earl had a lot of tough days – days with a lot of pain. But while he was battling for his life, he never lost his zest for living.

Talk about dealing with adversity and coming up big.

Earl came up big every day of his life. He chose how he was going to live. He loved hockey, he loved the Red Wings, and he loved life. His love of life and living was contagious and inspiring. He became a fixture in our dressing room. The players loved having him around. I talked to him a couple times a week. We talked a lot about hockey. We also talked about battling the disease, fighting it every day. If Earl called when I was in the truck, I put him on the speaker phone so my kids could hear him. He taught them what passion, "stick-to-it-iveness" and courage really meant. He taught me too.

One day last September, I got a text at 5:44 a.m. It was from Earl's brother Darby. It said, "Earl is in trouble. Please call." I called right away. Earl couldn't talk. His mom, Debbie, put the phone up to Earl's ear. I told Earl, "I'm proud of the fight you've fought. And now it's time for you to join my Mom, Beast, and Rusty in Heaven." (Beast – Brad McCrimmon – and Rusty – Ruslan Salei – were two former members of the Red Wings family who had just died in a plane crash in Russia with the Lokomotiv team.) I said to Earl, "They will look after you, and in turn you will look after us." After I put down the phone, I thought about how much Earl had given me, my family, and the Red Wings.

He died a few minutes after we hung up the phone.

Earl lived his entire life like it was an occasion. And he rose to it each and every day.

I miss you, my friend.

There's one other important element in coming up big I want to mention.

And that's fear. Fear can be a great motivator, depending what you choose to be scared of.

Personally, I don't fear failure. I know failure is a possibility, but it's just not what I'm afraid of.

But there is something I am afraid of.

I'm afraid of being just "good enough."

That fear keeps me activated. It keeps me grinding to get better.

It's a fear that's driven me since I was first hired in Red Deer. Maybe even before that. It's a fear that has helped me take every step in my career. It's a good kind of fear. It doesn't wear you out or paralyze you, it pushes you forward. It gets you in early and it keeps you trying new things. The fear of just good enough pushes you to be tough on yourself, no matter how good you might be getting.

Good enough gets you by. Good enough keeps things comfortable. Good enough keeps things familiar. But fear of just good enough can push you to be better. It can push you to break through and hit your potential – to make a difference. It can push you to success that at first seems unreachable.

Good enough is where you find average.

Just good enough will keep you right in the middle of the pack. And the middle of the pack is okay if that's where you want to be. A lot of people are happy there. But there are some things you should know about good enough.

Good enough won't help you find your potential.

Good enough isn't where the fun is.

Good enough doesn't come up big.

Good enough isn't where difference-makers come from.

Good enough won't get you to your dreams.

Good enough isn't where you find joy.

And good enough won't get you to the top of the podium.

If you live your life in fear that you're not going to get a chance, or fear that you haven't got what it takes, or fear of failing at what you do, those are fears that can paralyze you. Try being scared of something else.

Try being afraid of being average. If we had been average against the Russians, we would have never won that day. If we'd only been good enough, we would never have shut down Alexander Ovechkin.

Are you ready to be better than just good enough?

Sidney Crosby's quick shot beats US goalie Ryan Miller in overtime – the golden goal. (Jamie Squire/Getty Images Sport/Getty Images)

Sidney Crosby, about two seconds after taking that shot. Where were you when Sid scored? (Photo courtesy of Jeff Vinnick/Hockey Canada)

Roberto Luongo stoned the Slovaks in the last minute
to preserve Canada's 3–2 win in the semi-final game.
(Photo courtesy of Jeff Vinnick/Hockey Canada)

The only way to match it would be to dye your hair the colour of the flag and paint your face gold. (Photo courtesy of Jeff Vinnick/Hockey Canada)

Canada's entire gold medal team. Delivering on home ice created the moment of a lifetime. (Photo courtesy of Jeff Vinnick/Hockey Canada)

The management brain trust of Canada's gold medal team: Kevin Lowe, Ken Holland, Steve Yzerman, and Doug Armstrong. (Photo courtesy of Jeff Vinnick/Hockey Canada)

I think as I've gained more experience, I've become more open to other people's take on things. And one truth I've come to understand is that no matter how good you are, no matter how accomplished, you always learn by asking questions. And you can't lose by listening.

When you talk to a Scott Niedermayer, you learn. When you talk to a Jarome Iginla, you learn. When you talk to Ken Holland, General Manager of the Detroit Red Wings and a four-time winner of the Stanley Cup, or Doug Armstrong, Director of Player Personnel for the St. Louis Blues and a Stanley Cup winner, or Kevin Lowe, President of Hockey Operations for the Edmonton Oilers and a five-time winner of the Stanley Cup, you learn. You learn big time. I certainly did. Being surrounded by smart people only makes you better.

On top of everything else, the Olympics was a great learning experience for me.

If you are really intent on getting better, you have to look at every day as a chance to learn. When you're learning, you're getting better.

And when you keep getting better, you're getting yourself into position to win.

You can't be the best in the world without world-class dedication to practice.

It just doesn't happen any other way. And that means practicing smart, not just hard. Winning is in the details. Repetition accelerates learning. For any team, roles and responsibilities have to be crystal-clear.

Our team practices at the Olympics were high-tempo and demanding. We weren't doing drills for the sake of doing drills. We focused on structure and execution at maximum speed. We worked on what we needed to get after.

There was no fluff. It was all foundation-based.

Under pressure, you always fall back on foundation and structure. You always go back to who you are. That's why foundation and structure are so important. And it has to be ingrained in you if you're going to fall back on it. Who you are sets the foundation and the structure that allow you to properly execute. It frames the way you play in all zones. It sets up accountability, so each and every player can do their part.

Our game summary sheets reflect my belief in attention to detail. We chart the flow of a game and period-to-period situations meticulously. That is, the match-ups, the face-off percentages, the penalty kill and power-play success. We analyze it all. And analysis brings clarity to any adjustments needed within your game.

As I've said, when a team or player is under pressure, one of the key things a coach needs to do is focus on foundation. This ensures that everyone understands what needs to be done. This allows each player to execute at top speed – knowing and trusting that everyone else is doing their part.

When you bring in a group of talent that has to mesh quickly, what you're really asking the players to do is find their game within the team's game. They have to be clear on their particular role. Whether it's about the power play, the penalty kill, or a four-on-four situation, talent needs to be focused. The bigger the pressure, the more doubt and distraction can factor in; the bigger the need for structure, so skill can come out.

One practice that carried an extra importance was the one we had after losing to the USA, the practice before we played Germany.

We beat Germany 8–2.

But in reality, beginning with Germany, we were on track to play four "Game Sevens" in a row.

After the Germans would come the quarter-finals, the semi-finals and then the gold medal game. We were on track to play four games between February 23 and February 28.

So the practice before we faced the Germans, just one day after the loss to the USA, was important technically and emotionally.

Emotionally, we had to keep the team focused. We couldn't be distracted by the weight of the moment. I know it's a cliché to say that we had to take it one game at a time, but that was really the situation we were in. As much as everyone can get caught up in momentum and carry-over, I'm not a big believer in that. I'm a big believer in being prepared, getting focused, and executing. If you do all those things, you have a chance to get lucky. We just needed to play: to be ourselves, to do what we do.

As we got on the ice for practice, it was clear everybody was business-like, energized, and on task. That's the tone we were looking for.

We had a great practice. We continued to build on our foundation and structure so our players' individual skills would come through as we worked our way through the tournament.

There had been a lot of talk in the press about my experimenting with lines in the previous three games. In particular, the "issue" of finding the wingers for Sidney Crosby was a hot topic of media debate. For me, and Sid, it was never about finding the best wingers for him. What it was about was finding ways to win and get better as a team. I talked to Sid about it. I asked him what he thought. That's something I might never have done as a young coach, but as a leader you have to be confident enough to ask questions. By asking questions, you get to the best answer. You have to be confident enough to let your team, your players, own part of the process.

It would pay off big time through the rest of the games.

Prior to the game against Germany, we decided to put Eric Staal and Jerome Iginla on a line flanking Crosby. And against Germany, we dominated. Iginla scored two goals, Crosby added one, and Staal had two assists.

Like I say, you have to keep learning.

Do you look at every day as an opportunity to learn?

CHAPTER 10

33 MILLION CANADIANS

No matter how big you dream, how committed or intense you are, I believe you miss out if you don't enjoy the process.

We went to Vancouver to win Olympic gold. Absolutely.

I believe we also went to Vancouver to experience the Olympic Games. To have fun. To feel the energy. To soak in the national pride. To be among our fellow Canadians and visitors from around the world.

I loved the Olympic journey. I loved that my family loved it. I loved that every single person in Vancouver seemed to love it.

I think the volunteers did a great job representing our country; welcoming the world. Being there and being a part of the games made me genuinely appreciate all the time and effort it took to make the experience possible. Talk about difference-makers, talk about unsung heroes – the Olympic volunteers were something special.

The energy and spontaneity in Vancouver were inspiring. The singing of the national anthem on the streets and the exchanging of jerseys with total strangers symbolized the spirit and fun of the games.

Enjoying the ride is a big part of living.

Interestingly, for me, one of the best parts of the Olympic journey didn't happen in Vancouver.

The press conference announcing the lineup of the Canadian Olympic team was something I'll remember for the rest of my life.

It took place in Saskatoon, the city where I grew up. It was a great place to grow up. My Dad and two of my sisters still call it home. It's a vibrant, progressive city that is home to the University of Saskatchewan. It was the home town of the great Gordie Howe. I played minor hockey at Kinsmen Arena – not far from Gordie Howe Bowl, a football stadium named for the hockey hero, which says something about the respect he holds in Saskatchewan.

Saskatoon is known as the City of Bridges. As you fly in, you can't help but notice the old Canadian National hotel, the Bessborough, set on the banks of the South Saskatchewan River. It's really beautiful. I belonged to the water-ski club and used to water-ski on that river as a kid. For me, coming in for the press conference brought back a lot of great memories. In January 2010, as I flew in for the event, ice covering the river and snow everywhere in sight, I couldn't help but smile.

It could have been a postcard.

The press conference was in Saskatoon because it was hosting the World Junior Hockey Championships.

The World Juniors also brings back a lot of great memories for me. In 1997 I was coach of the Canadian junior team that won a gold medal in Geneva, Switzerland. I will always remember the players standing arm-in-arm singing our national anthem after a great gold-medal win over the USA. I thought to myself how great it would be to relive that moment in Vancouver in February 2010.

I'll always be grateful to Kenny Holland, my GM in Detroit and one of the key guys on the Olympic management team, for encouraging me to make the trip to Saskatoon. The Red Wings had a game the next night and I was thinking I'd have to pass on the press conference. I mean, it was a press conference, and I had work to do. I had a practice to run. Bottom line, I get paid to win games for the Detroit Red Wings.

Kenny reminded me of a few things. One, it was the press conference announcing the roster of the Canadian Olympic hockey team. Two, I was the head coach of that team. And three, it was all happening in my home town with my Dad, two of my sisters, and three of my nieces there in person.

The press conference at the Saskatoon Training Centre was something special. The place was packed and buzzing with energy. I looked around and felt an overwhelming sense of support. I saw a lot of local people I hadn't seen in years. I was very proud and humbled at the same time.

It's impossible to describe how much it meant to me.

I believe that when we look back at our lives, what we will remember most are the moments. Days, weeks, months, and sometimes even years can blur in our memories. But moments with family and with friends are so important. Times when we feel joy, gratitude, and pride are irreplaceable.

As busy as we are, we can't become too busy to live.

No matter how successful, powerful, or well-intentioned we are, nobody can get back a missed moment.

The press conference reminded me that the Olympics opportunity would be a "moment" for me.

I needed to experience and enjoy it all. I promised myself that when we got to Vancouver, I'd have fun along the way.

One thing I did to keep my promise came after our first game. Maybe it seems like a little thing, but it made a big impact on my Olympic experience. I told the coaches I was going to start walking back and forth from the ice rink to the Olympic Village. I got Jacques Lemaire and Lindy Ruff to walk with me every game. It was about a fifteen-minute walk. I wanted to experience the excitement and energy of the people.

It was fun. It energized us. People were *alive*. We fed off them. You could see and feel their passion. Their energy was awesome. They made us feel like they were part of our team. People were enjoying the moment.

And so was I. It was great to be among them.

Are you making the most of the moments in your life?

CHAPTER 11

HOME ICE IS AN ADVANTAGE

You can either embrace pressure or it can own you.

Hosting the Olympics, playing on home ice was something special.

People talked about it adding pressure. And it did. Playing for your country is different. The stakes are different. The sense of pride is different. It's not only about what you do – it's about who you are. It's about who we are as Canadians. People had put their faith in me, our staff, and our players. We had to make a decision to embrace and enjoy it or let the pressure crush us.

We chose to embrace it. If you want to reach your dreams you have to gravitate towards pressure. We are all capable of it. It's a choice. It's what you have to do. Being in the right place at the right time isn't just about being lucky. It's about choosing to be there.

If you want to be great, be accountable. If you want to be a part of something great, be accountable.

Home ice shines a bright light on that. Do your job so your team can do theirs. If you really want to hold yourself accountable, do your job when high expectations meet a big opportunity. Embracing pressure means delivering when it matters most.

Accountability is the No. 1 word in team sports. It's the No. 1 word in the world of business.

I think accountability is important in every aspect of what we do. In our house, we have something called "Kitchen Table Accountability" – it's a higher level of accountability that comes from those who know you best, those who love you. It comes with trust, comfort, and the assumption of positive intent. And it just tends to happen at dinnertime around the kitchen table. If you get too full of yourself or too far ahead of yourself, it's the kind of accountability that keeps you in line. If you try to stretch the truth or make the mistake of saying something stupid, you get called on it. It's the kind of accountability that calls "b.s." out on the table. It's about holding each other to the kind of people we should be.

Nothing is more important to me than my family. We support each other. We encourage each other. We love each other.

And we make each other accountable.

In sports, as in business, difference-makers understand pressure.

It simply means you have a chance.

Find pressure, and you'll find opportunity to make a difference and contribute. Try to take your business to the next level, your students to the next level, your charity to the next level or your team to the next level. And when you do that, you'll find pressure. You'll also find the chance to do something better, to do something meaningful.

Pressure comes in many forms – physical, mental, emotional. You can feel it in big ways or small.

Pressure can prop open the door for doubt. The greater the pressure, the more open the door to doubt can be. When doubt lingers, it becomes your opponent – more so than the other team. And big doubt is a formidable opponent. When a team or individual allows the pressure to get the better of them, they tighten up. It can paralyze them. You can see it in every aspect of their game or performance. You can't perform if you're tight. And when you don't perform, doubt grows.

Some people shy away from pressure. Some people fold. They let pressure get the better of them.

Again, you have a choice.

People who chase their dreams learn to want pressure; they learn to make pressure work for them. Pressure can drive us to prepare more, commit more, focus more, and do more. Commitment, focus, and preparation can all work to push us beyond our doubt. Ultimately, you earn the right to feel good about your preparation. And when you get beyond doubt you relax, execute, and perform at your highest level.

As a team, we were under more pressure to perform than any other individual or team at the 2010 Olympics. We were under as much pressure as any Canadian Olympian had ever been. Of course we were aware of that pressure and we could feel it. But we never allowed it to get the better of us.

We would play to our potential.

Everybody has potential. It isn't something limited to a special few.

But the first thing you have to do to reach your potential is realize you *have* it.

Meeting your potential and fulfilling your dreams are closely linked. The truth is, if you don't maximize your potential, chances are you're not going to fulfil your dreams. That's the math. When you're working to your potential, you're chasing your dreams.

Many people leave a lot of their potential on the table. And many people fall short of their dreams. All of us have dreams inside of us, inside wanting to get out, a belief in what could be. Your dreams don't have to make you famous. They don't have to make you rich. They don't have to win you awards. All your dreams have to do is bring out your best. And that will be good for everybody.

A professor of mine at McGill University, John Chomay, talked a lot about potential and was a big influence on me. I was enrolled in the Faculty of Education and he was my supervisor for student teaching. He was a true educator. He was interested in his students. He wanted them to learn and grow. I loved going into his office and just talking. He cared about me. He invested time in me. I still appreciate what he did for me.

At the end of my teaching "practicum," he told me he was going to give me the highest mark he had ever given any student. He gave me the grade but told me it came with an obligation to live up to my potential.

What he said was pretty clear: "At this point, what you have is only potential. Don't waste it. Maximize what you've been given."

Potential is an empty promise until you activate it.

Or in Professor Chomay's words, "Potential is simply a dirty word if you don't live up to it." And activating potential takes commitment. It's a commitment to bring your best to your job, your team, your business, your cause, or your community. And it's energy-giving. It will energize you and those around you.

It's important to remember that potential is a moving target. I don't believe you are ever a finished product. And you have to keep re-evaluating what your potential is. The potential I had twenty years ago, ten years ago, five years ago is different from the potential I have today. You have to keep growing. You have to keep stretching. Change is a constant. If you don't evolve you will be left behind. And that's true no matter how accomplished you are. Ask anybody who has achieved something and they'll say it's easier to get to the top than to stay there. If you want to stay on top, you have to keep stretching the limits of your potential.

I try to measure up to Professor Chomay's challenge every day of my life. Every single day. There are good and bad days. Some days I come up short, but I try not to waste any of them. The best way not to waste your potential is to work at it. And the harder you work at it, the better your chance of having your potential work for you.

An interesting thing happens when you're working to meet your potential: fun happens. In my experience, working to meet your potential fills your life with joy.

Pressure helps to maximize your potential and, in the end, increase your joy.

Think of pressure as a tool – one that you shouldn't keep locked away in your toolbox.

Consider the situation.

The Olympics are in Canada. We have the organization to win. We have the talent to win. We have the team to win. There are great expectations. Anything short of gold is going to be seen as a failure. Losing would be seen as a disaster. Lots of pressure. But we have a chance.

That's a great thing, right? All you want is a chance. All you need is a chance.

As we got past Russia, and headed into the "final four," the talk of our potential and the intensity of expectations were only getting higher.

How close are you to hitting your potential?

CHAPTER 12

NOTHING CAN DISTRACT US

As an organization, Hockey Canada had a singular focus.

We were going to be the best in the world. And we were going to win the gold medal to prove it.

I think relationships are critical to an organization or a team's success. It's important to know, trust and respect the people around you. That kind of connection allows you to focus on the important stuff.

It was important to me that the relationship I had with Steve Yzerman was anchored in mutual respect. I respect Steve as a person and as a family guy. He's a great leader and his knowledge of our game is second to none. From the minute I got the job, we knew how to work together, which was great. We had a lot of big decisions ahead.

We hit the ground running immediately at the NHL draft in Montreal in June 2009, when we announced that Jacques Lemaire, Lindy Ruff, and Ken Hitchcock would join our coaching staff. After the announcement, I asked Steve if I could have a little bit of time with the coaches. I grabbed some beer, found a white board, and got the four of us together. We talked players, forechecking, controlling the neutral zone, and defensive-zone structure. We talked the game.

And I'll tell you, that is about as good of a coaching clinic as you can get. What an experience – to be sharing ideas right off the start with hockey minds of their calibre.

Some people cautioned me about sharing too much. Their thinking was, if you share your "secrets," you'll lose your competitive advantage in the NHL. If you share all your insight and learning, you lose your edge. I didn't think like that. Neither did my coaches. I wasn't going to hold anything back. And I figured if my thinking got out around the league, well, I'd just have to push myself to think differently, to think smarter. You have to continually evolve and get better. I'm about the next thing.

Being about the next thing is a good thing.

The session in Montreal set us up well for the coaches' camp in Vancouver in July. Going in, I think we all figured we'd do some socializing, a little golfing and get to know each other, but that wasn't the way it was at all. We worked tirelessly. We spent hours every day setting up our curriculum for the summer camp with the players that would come later. The coaches' camp provided us the foundation of what we were going to teach and ingrain into the players. It was the foundation we would carry into the Olympics. We wanted to immerse the players in it at their camp, so they would be familiar with it the first time we stepped onto the ice in Vancouver.

Jacques' experience and teaching ability, Lindy's energy and offensive-minded perspective on the game, and Hitch's attention to detail and understanding of process worked well together from beginning to end.

It was a best-in-class operation.

When we got to the players' summer camp, we hit it out of the park. It was a five-day camp in Calgary in August 2009. Our preparation really paid off. We were so organized and structured, there was no time wasted. We brought in 46 players – you need two full teams for a good camp. And the commitment of the players we brought into camp was amazing. The pace of that summer camp was like a Stanley Cup final. It was unbelievable.

Any successful group, team, or organization has to be built on commitment to each other.

Team Canada had that.

We were focused on a common goal.

We were focused on bringing the best ideas.

We were focused on being the best team in the world.

Of the 46 players who came to our summer camp, half of them would not make the final cut. As coaches, part of our focus was seeing who worked together best. There were incredibly tough choices to be made. In fact, the exact lineup of 23 players wasn't agreed until the morning of the press conference in January when we announced the team.

The final forward chosen for the team was a big debate. We had some passionate discussions for a while around our final choice. There were strong opinions as to who the last guy should be. This was about representing your country at the Olympic Games and choosing from among the very best hockey talent in the world. Nobody took any part of the selection process lightly, but when it came down to deciding on the final roster spot, the level of commitment and passion toward getting it right was clear.

At 6 a.m. on the day of the press conference, I was lying in bed in my room at the Bessborough when I got a text from Steve Yzerman.

It read "Are you up?" I responded: "I'm a coach, I'm always up."

The first thing we did was agree on the final forward. The management team had given us their thoughts and handed them over to Steve and me to make the final call.

We were aligned and confident in our decision.

Focus is fundamental.

But focus can cut two ways. I believe you can "over-focus." And over-focusing can get you out of focus. If you focus on one thing, everything else can start to blur. A singular focus, over time, isn't really living. At least the way I see it, you miss too much by focusing on one thing – no matter what the thing is. Life has a lot to offer. You want to experience as much as you can.

Over-focusing can hurt performance.

You can't analyze, strategize, and grind all the time. Day in, day out. It'll wear you down. It'll wear your team down. It will wear down the people around you. That doesn't mean you're not committed or that you lack the right intensity. It means you're a human being. It's okay to change up your focus.

Performance-wise, it's tough to execute when you can't relax or when the only thing you are is on task. I've known a lot of coaches and people in business who believed that if you aren't on task, you're wasting your time. I disagree. To me the answer is being in the moment, whatever the moment is.

Changing your focus isn't being distracted. Changing your focus can be an energy-giving activity.

In Vancouver, when we were meeting, practicing, and playing, that's what we were doing – meeting, practicing, and playing. And when we were doing it, that's what we were focused on. But it was fantastic to have our families with us in Vancouver. The 4:30 p.m. game times were great because they allowed us to have our nights free to be with our families and the families of the other players and coaches. We became part of a bigger family. We had a blast at Hockey Canada House.

Sharing the Olympic experience with family enriched it beyond belief. When I wasn't doing my job, I was a fan just like everybody else. I could enjoy and exhale. Everyone needs to breathe.

Our families helped us relax and get away from the pressure of the games. Nothing took us off task. And being with our families helped keep us fresh and loose. It gave all the management, coaches and players a real break – emotionally. It shifted us away from the pressure of the Games. It saved our energy and gave us something fun to do and think about away from the game. I think being able to share the bigger Olympic experience with our families, changing up our focus, helped us win the gold.

A distraction? No way. A different focus, a change of pace? Yes.

Moments to remember? For sure.

I think we need to have more than one focus in our life. It's just a healthy way to live.

Chasing our dreams isn't about having tunnel vision.

Putting all our energy into one thing, all the time, every day is limiting. There's a lot to enjoy in this world. Changing up your focus once in a while opens us up to new experiences. That's never a bad thing. And it'll never get in the way of us reaching our dreams.

The key is that you've got to focus on one thing at a time. Be all-in to what you're doing, when you're doing it.

At the same time you've got to keep your eyes open to new experiences, new ways of thinking, new ways of doing things. Soaking in all life has to offer will make you better at what you do.

You never know where inspiration, learning, and growth will come from.

Is your life truly in focus?

CHAPTER 13

NOTHING WILL STOP US

Life's speed bumps should never stop us – they should only help us go forward a little smarter.

I've been to the Stanley Cup finals three times. I've won once. I've lost twice in Game Seven. You want to talk about speed bumps? That's a tough way to lose. To have a chance to win it all means a lot. It takes a lot too – it takes winning 15 playoff games to get there. It's an incredible process. You learn, you grow, you get better and stronger through the playoff process. The stakes are higher. The learning curve is steeper. The more you go through it, the better you are. That's why you compete.

When I was coaching in Anaheim and we lost in the Stanley Cup finals to New Jersey, it was devastating. To work so hard, to play so well, and to get so close was beyond devastating. After addressing the players post-game, I came out of the dressing room, stood behind the bench and watched the Devils celebrate their Stanley Cup victory. I took it all in. I watched Scott Stevens, the New Jersey captain, lift the Cup over his head and take his victory lap around the rink. I watched the players and coaches slap each other on the back and hug one another. I watched as they smiled, laughed, and stood proud alongside the Stanley Cup.

I'm not sure if I went out there because I wanted to know how good it could feel or how bad it felt.

Either way, I knew I would be back. I knew my time would come.

I knew I would get my hands on the Cup.

The chance to test yourself against the best accelerates everything.

The bigger the setback, the tougher the loss, the more you want the prize. Setbacks shouldn't stop you, they should fuel your push towards your goals and dreams.

Obsessing over falling short or messing up is toxic. It generates negative energy. Negativity fosters doubt. Negativity is heavy. It weighs you down. It's counterproductive. Negativity is an energy-taker. It saps your strength. It's contagious and nobody is immune. You have to find a way to stay strong and overcome it. And overcome it completely.

Oftentimes, in the end, it comes down to a matter of will. There's no real magic to it.

On the subject of magic, I get asked a lot about my McGill tie and about being superstitious. Am I a little superstitious? Yes. Do I believe luck controls the outcome of a game? No. I believe hard work is the best way to get lucky. And I know superstition won't help you battle negativity or doubt. But I do like to wear my McGill tie for big games. I guess it's a ritual that started as a way of saying thanks to a university that helped me along my journey. It's a great school. I'm a proud graduate of McGill. But the tie "works" because of the skill and heart of the players and people around me.

That said, its record is very good.

I think the power of our will resides in our "drive train." We all have one. And, I believe, we all have a stronger drive train, a stronger will to succeed, than we think. We have more to give than we give ourselves credit for. Remind yourself of that once in a while.

Sometimes the strength we require is physical, sometimes mental. Sometimes it's emotional, sometimes spiritual. In order to get to this greater strength, you've got to push your boundaries, challenge yourself to get outside your comfort zone. Your drive train gets bigger and stronger every time you push yourself and put it to the test. The harder you push, the more powerful your drive train becomes – your will to succeed gets stronger the more you put it to the test.

And, in the end, the better you feel about who you are.

That's been my experience.

It has also been my experience that your passion tends to go toward the things you're good at.

If you don't love what you do, you won't be good at it. And you really have to be aware and honest with yourself that you may not be as good as you think you are – because sometimes a setback can be a springboard to a better opportunity.

I grew up playing hockey. Like almost every kid from Canada who grows up playing hockey, I had dreams of making it to the NHL. I played in juniors and four years of college hockey while I was at McGill. I was a decent college player – I got named to a couple of all-star teams and played for Canada in the 1985 World Student Games. I got a tryout with the Vancouver Canucks in 1986. The tryout was a great experience, but I knew I wasn't an NHL-calibre player. I wasn't talented enough to play at that level. I had to be honest with myself about that. Tom Watt, the Canucks coach, called me in and asked me what I was going to do next. He was happy to hear that I was going back to grad school at McGill. He actually let me stay a few extra days at the hotel so I could experience Expo 86. It was unbelievable.

But as that door closed, my passion for hockey took me in another direction. It set me on the road towards being a coach. Coaching is something I'm good at. Coaching is something I love.

And passion can make you unstoppable.

That said, chasing your dreams isn't easy. I've been fired in Moose Jaw, taken over a program on the verge of extinction in Lethbridge, and could barely pay the monthly bills when I first coached in Spokane. People refer to me now as a successful head coach in the NHL, but the road getting there took some time, determination, and perseverance. Success didn't happen overnight.

Overnight success only looks like "overnight" to the people who don't know.

It hasn't happened without obstacles or adversity. I've had my share of speed bumps. Truth is, no matter what you've accomplished, the speed bumps never stop coming. And that's okay, that's life. It makes things interesting. It makes things exciting.

Ultimately it can make things great.

There's one more truth to be told.

I couldn't have got to where I am in my journey without my wife Rene.

You know the old saying that behind every successful man there is a good woman. Well, I'm living proof that it's true, except for one thing. My wife has never stood behind me. She has always stood beside me. She's given me balance, perspective, and support. She's been my partner through it all. She's one of my inspirations. She's a strong, smart woman who, like my Mom, is intent on raising good kids who work hard to make a difference.

Strength of will is a personal thing, but at points in time we all need help. She has been that help.

My kids – Allie, Michael, and Taylor – help me too.

My wife and my children energize me every time I'm running low. They give me the fuel to keep me going. I'm so grateful for my family. And oftentimes I feel they give me so much more than I can ever give back.

If it's been a while since you thanked your family for all the support they offer you every single day, now might be a good time to do it.

Without my family, I wouldn't have the fuel I need to chase my dreams.

When all is said and done, you can't get around it. At some level, taking charge of your dreams is an act of will.

We know being tested is all part of the deal. The option to stop is always there. Don't take it.

It's not easy. The best things don't come easy.

This is a big one for me. Getting what you want without earning it is hollow. It doesn't make you stronger. Getting things easily isn't always a good thing. It doesn't help maximize your potential.

Besides, the process of improving is fun. The feeling of progress is fun.

You shouldn't want easy. Nothing easy is worth having. Easy is no risk. Easy is no growth. Easy is no learning. And, most importantly, easy is no fun. Easy is just standing still.

Go hard and you can create the ride of your life.

How easily are you stopped on the way to chasing your dreams?

CHAPTER 14

OUR DETERMINATION WILL DEFINE US

For me, determination has always been about doing, not saying.

It's easy to talk.

Delivering is a different thing. You can't deliver anything of meaning unless you're determined.

There are a lot of people who are determined enough to be there until it gets hard. You know these people. You've seen them in action (or inaction) at your office, your school, your PTA meetings, at team practices or in a big game.

The reality is that when you're chasing a dream, you've got to go until there's no doubt.

Our semi-final against Slovakia was a case in point.

The Slovaks were a surprise, having made it through to the semi-finals. They were capable of playing the kind of defensive game that could cause us problems. They had stars like Zdeno Chara, Marian Hossa, and Marian Gaborik, and they were coming off a huge emotional win against the Swedes.

And with us coming off a huge emotional win, the game against Slovakia had a unique challenge to it. You're playing both against a revved-up opposition and your own mindset. Slovakia was a good team but we were expected to win. A lot of people in the media and the stands were looking beyond Slovakia in anticipation of the gold medal game. We weren't. We knew it would be a test. We'd go into the game with the same focus and urgency. And for 50 of the 60 minutes we were getting it done. We were up 3–0 after the second period.

But nothing is pre-ordained.

Early in the third period, when the Canadian fans started chanting "We want the USA!", I said to myself, "It's too soon, too soon."

Hearing those chants scared me as much as I've ever been scared in my life.

The Slovaks scored two goals in the third period.

All of a sudden we had a 3–2 game with five minutes left to play.

You can't let outcome get in the way of process. You can't get ahead of yourself. It can be a hard thing to do. Put another way, you can't hold the Cup over your head while you're playing game. You need the stick in your hands until the final horn goes.

We got ahead of ourselves against the Slovaks. They pulled their goalie in the last minute and almost completed the comeback. But we hung in there. And sometimes that's what you have to do. Great teams tend to do it more than people realize.

In Detroit, we won 50 games – out of an 82-game season – four years in a row. Over the summer, people somehow start to think that you won every game 10–1. Truth is, you have to win a lot of one-goal games to be successful. And a lot of those aren't pretty.

Here at the Olympics, our 3–2 win against Slovakia got us into the gold medal game. We did what we needed to do. We grinded it out. Champions do that.

Sure it would have been great to win 3–0, but the huge save Lou made in the last minute against Slovakia gave him some real confidence going into the final game against the Americans and their goalie Ryan Miller. It gave us some real confidence too.

We weren't carrying any doubt as we headed into the gold medal game.

Good teams have skill. Great teams have skill and heart.

— — ·—

When you chase your dreams, you have to drive beyond what I call the "give-in line."

Dreams don't meet you halfway. It doesn't work that way.

Determination fuels you. A lack of determination sucks you dry. And you can come up short.

We can all feel the give-in line when we are being pushed close to our limits. It's when we start to ask "Is this worth it?" It's when we start to feel that there has to be another way. Crossing the give-in line accelerates us along the path to our dreams. It's a line that tests our determination, our drive train.

Think about a marathon when you hit mile 22. That's the folding mark – the challenge can become too much, too hard, too overwhelming. To finish the marathon, you have to push through the give-in line.

The give-in line is more than just a physical thing. It's a mental, emotional and spiritual thing. And it can show itself in the middle of a big project at work, in a fundraising initiative for a local charity, or in the context of providing care and comfort for someone in desperate need. You know the line when you feel it. Once you hit the line, there are really only two choices – give in or go on.

Dreaming with your eyes open helps you see your goal clearly and push through.

Achieving your dreams demands a decision to cross the line.

Do you go beyond the give-in line?

CHAPTER 15

WE ARE BUILT TO WIN

We all have to build toward our dreams.

And dreams like Olympic hockey gold don't happen without a lot of work, from a lot of people.

One thing that Steve and I share is a belief in doing your homework. Nobody would out-prepare us.

That's critical because when you are playing the best of the best, success is in the margins. Everything counts. Everything makes a difference. Every detail is important. Small differences can have a big impact – 211 degrees is hot water, 212 degrees is steam. And that can drive a locomotive. One degree more from a goalie, a defenceman, or anyone in the organization can put you over the top.

Throughout my career I've learned a lot from different people. I tend to learn more from what they do than what they say. Before I got to the NHL my coaching philosophy was pretty well established. I've progressed as a coach since getting to the league, but my beliefs are still the same.

I was fortunate enough early in my career to compete against some great coaches. I coached against guys like Perry Pearn, Billy Moores, and Don Hay. All of them are great at what they do. They were all the best in their leagues at the time I competed against them.

Pearn was at the Northern Alberta Institute of Technology; he went on to be an assistant coach with four different NHL teams. From him I learned the importance of being organized and paying attention to detail. Moores was at the University of Alberta; now he's with the Edmonton Oilers. From him I learned the importance of demanding excellence in execution, what it took to perform at a high level, and how to treat players right. Hay was with the Kamloops Blazers; he went on to work as a head coach in Phoenix and Calgary. From him I learned the importance of teaching, of repetition in learning, and knowing how to break things down and make them understandable.

I brought absolutely everything I learned into my Team Canada experience. As I said, I shared everything because it gave us the best chance to win. The same was true for Jacques, Lindy, and Hitch.

Discipline, attention to detail and doing your homework are keys to success. The other guy is doing his homework too – and knowing that you've made the proper commitment to preparation can overcome doubt.

No team would outwork us.

Every single person on the management team and coaching staff for Team Canada shared a world class work ethic and a relentless desire to excel. Our hours of analysis in selecting the final 23 players who travelled to Vancouver were proof of this belief. It was the kind of day-in, day-out hard work that doesn't have a lot of glory attached to it.

We shattered the give-in line. The grinding work we did was invaluable in our preparation to win gold.

Not only did a lot of effort go into the selection process – watching games, breaking down films, debating players' strengths and weaknesses – there was a lot of pride involved: personal pride, professional pride, and national pride.

By harnessing so much pride of our own, we would give our country a team to be proud of.

We were determined to make this the best hockey team to ever play for Canada.

We knew it would be a total team effort.

That's what it would take. That's what it always takes. And that's what makes team competition so special.

We would ask every player to find their own game within our team's game. Even though we had a great players' camp in the summer of 2009, pulling a team together in the middle of the NHL season would demand every member of the organization – management, coaches, and players – do their part and accept their role, so we could be great together. We knew we were bringing together a group of individuals who had to become a team in a hurry.

To win the gold medal, we didn't need the best collection of talent. We needed the best team.

Whether it's winning Olympic gold or building your dream company, whether it's getting into your dream school or dreaming of how to make the world a better place, you don't do it alone.

Ever.

Do you surround yourself with people who make you better?

CHAPTER 16

A TEAM OF CHARACTER

You can't cheat your way to your dreams.

If you want to live your dreams and make a difference, you have to do things with integrity. Shortcuts get you lost.

I've mentioned respect before, but I believe it's so important in everything we do.

You have to respect the process. You have to respect yourself. You have to respect the game. You have to respect the competition. And you have to respect your team. I think that respecting other people is essential – in sports and in life. Respect is a key to character.

A great way to respect other people is to give back. As I mentioned, my Mom died of cancer at 51. I saw a strong woman physically ravaged by the disease before it took her life. Cancer had never been a part of my life until then. But my Mom's battle, along with having two close friends lose young sons to the disease some years back, convinced me it was time to get involved.

That's how I met Earl Cook. And I've met a lot of other great kids along the way.

It's a cause I will always be involved in.

Cancer is a brutal thing, but when kids get cancer it becomes almost indescribably difficult. If I can raise money by headlining fundraising efforts, that's great. I'm happy to help. In July 2010, people in my home town of Saskatoon declared a Mike Babcock Day to kickstart the fundraising for the new Children's Hospital. Ken Holland, Todd McLellan (now the head coach at San Jose), and Scotty Bowman were in attendance. I was honoured to be a part of it. The sponsors and volunteers worked tirelessly to put a great day together. It was inspiring to be around a group of people so driven to do good; so driven to help make things better.

Talk about people who make a difference.

For me, giving back is about more than giving my name. It has to be about giving my time. I want to spend time with the kids. I want those kids to feel special. I want them to feel important. The truth is that without even knowing it, they give more to me than I ever could to them.

In 2008, after I coached the Red Wings to the Stanley Cup, the first place I took the Cup was to the Children's Hospital of Michigan in Detroit. Those kids' eyes lit up when they saw the Stanley Cup. It was a thrill for them, and an unforgettable moment for me. It was a very humbling experience. Spending time with kids who are battling cancer teaches you about what real adversity is. It teaches you courage and character. It really helps to put a lot of things into perspective. It reminds you to count your blessings.

It's interesting to me that the more you give back, the more you seem to get back.

Integrity is about who we really are. It's about what you really value.

Throughout a lifetime, that means having the ability to get outside of your body and take a look. You're not the picture on the mantel in the living room. That's probably been digitally refinished or retouched. Nothing or no one is picture-perfect. It's important to take a real look at yourself. See yourself through the eyes of your children, your parents, your players, or your colleagues. It can be an eye-opener, and sometimes what you see isn't what you had hoped.

Someone once told me that courage is about not lying to yourself.

I thought that was an interesting perspective. It makes you think differently about the decisions you make – how you behave under pressure, how you respond in leadership moments, how you treat those close to you and those around you. You have to look at yourself, and often you have to make adjustments. We all need to make adjustments. Life is about continual adjustment.

And you have to be willing to pursue feedback. It's difficult. It takes character.

To me, integrity means you're all-in. You're committed, not just when it looks good or when you think you have to be. You're committed in the quiet moments, at the hard times, to the "on your own" challenges. It means you're fully committed to the goal and the dream. You're willing to give whatever you have to contribute.

As a hockey coach, there are only two things that disappoint me. One is failure to prepare. And two is failure to compete. I imagine that's much the same for leaders in any profession. To execute and compete, you need the full-on commitment of yourself first, your leadership or management group second, and your people and players third.

In all my years of coaching I don't think I've met a player whose intention it was to disappoint. If you are disappointed with how your group or team is performing, the first person you should look at is yourself. Alignment and direction start at the top.

That's why it's called leadership.

Like I've said, competing at the highest level is an everyday commitment.

Do you think Shea Weber or Jonathan Toews are part-time performers?

No way.

What about people we've never heard of who are making a difference in their communities, schools, and in the lives of people less fortunate than themselves? The volunteer who keeps a music program alive in the face of unrelenting budget cuts, the nurse who rocks cancer-stricken babies to sleep at the local hospice, or the single mom working two jobs to give her kids a chance at a better life? You think they turn it on and off? You think their commitment disappears when things get difficult?

No way.

It's interesting with people who are committed to achieving their dreams: their commitment actually grows with the difficulty of the task.

I'm sure most of you have experienced the feeling of accomplishment that comes with something that took everything you had. Something that looked really difficult. Something that felt close to impossible. You got it done and you felt proud. You got it done because your commitment got stronger. Each and every day your commitment grew. And I'll bet you loved the process and took great joy from it. People driving toward their dreams want the challenge. They love the challenge. They seek out the challenge.

Everyone else finds themselves being just good enough.

I've talked about it before, but I think there are a lot of people who stop at good enough. These people have a "good enough meter" in their head and heart. They know when they've hit good enough and they stop. They find their comfort zone and stay put.

Why is it that the kid who sets out to get himself a B in math seems to always get that B in math?

Not one player on Team Canada had a good enough meter. They were a team of big dreamers and big doers. Team Canada was a team of character.

Go ahead. Dream bigger.

If you're not making a difference, what are you making?

CHAPTER 17

A TEAM OF DESTINY

The day before our gold medal game, I went to see the gold medal curling match with my family.

I could have been holed up in my room re-watching tape, reviewing the match-ups again, or over-analyzing the game plan. I could have, but I didn't. We had done the work. We knew we were ready. I knew I was ready. So my family went to the curling match. And we had so much fun. Curling doesn't have a reputation for thrills, but I think it was the most exciting sporting event I had ever seen. The crowd was so into it.

Late in the match, my wife said we should leave early to beat the crowd. I said, "Are you crazy?" I couldn't leave. I thought it was a foreshadowing of the day to come. All three medal teams were bagpiped past us. The Canadian skip, Kevin Martin, came by and gave me a nod as if to say "Tomorrow it's your turn."

Talk about inspiring. Talk about energizing.

Some people talked about destiny – it's one of those words that gets thrown around a lot in sports, and in life.

I don't believe your destiny is pre-determined.

There was no guarantee that "tomorrow" was going to be our day.

Destiny is something you create.

Destiny didn't score in the shoot-out against Switzerland. Destiny didn't dominate the Russians. And destiny didn't jump off the bench and help us beat the Slovaks.

Destiny didn't get us into the gold medal game.

Kevin Martin talks about something that I think can help create your destiny – the "extra mile club." Kevin Martin is the best skip in the world. He sets a standard for work ethic that is world-class. He's a machine. He has ice water running through his veins. He delivers when it matters. It's an inspiration to watch him compete.

A lot of people think they prepare. A lot of people think they work hard. But it takes a commitment to go that extra mile to be ready when your moment arrives.

What often separates people who reach their goals from those who fall short is the will to push past their comfort zone. It takes a special level of dedication to go that extra mile. The same is true in every area of your life. You can stop when things become uncomfortable – physically or mentally – convinced that you have done as much as you can do. Or you can push a little harder and take yourself a little farther.

That's what it takes.

When I coached the Red Wings to the Stanley Cup in 2008 we had a team of "extra milers." Up and down that lineup we had a group of players, coaches, and management that pushed harder, prepared more, and committed to winning in a way that made us a team on a mission. Game in and game out, we were a machine. Setbacks just made us work harder. Adversity simply made us stronger.

We also had – and still do have – the best owners in professional sports. Mike and Marian Ilitch have a record of success that is second to none – four Stanley Cups and twenty consecutive play-off appearances. They have created a family atmosphere anchored in support and respect for all – from the people selling the tickets, to those cleaning the stands and driving Zambonis – we are all a part of it. They expect and demand success. And they have set a very high bar in terms of what success looks like. But they give their people the tools and opportunity to be successful. It's a rare thing. And it's all you can ask for.

In 2007, we got knocked out by Anaheim but we had what it took to get there. In 2008, leaders like Nick Lidstrom, Pavel Datsyuk, Henrik Zetterberg, and Kris Draper wouldn't allow us to fall short. We won the Jennings Trophy (Dominik Hasek and Chris Osgood for best goaltending), we won the Norris Trophy (Nick Lidstrom for best defenceman), we won the Lady Byng Trophy (Pavel Datsyuk for most gentlemanly player), we won the Frank Selke Trophy (Pavel Datsyuk for best defensive forward), we won the President's Trophy (for most points in the regular season), we won the Conn Smythe Trophy (Henrik Zetterberg for playoff MVP) – and we won it all to earn the Stanley Cup. Those Red Wings and their fans did it, individually and collectively, by going the extra mile.

Going into the gold medal game in Vancouver, I knew we had a team of extra milers. I'd seen it before. I knew what a team of extra milers looked like. I knew what it felt like. The Americans had beaten us once. It wasn't going to happen again. Team Canada was going the extra mile.

Dream chasers never depend on destiny being there. We were ready to create our own. No doubt.

What are you doing to create your destiny?

CHAPTER 18

LET THE WORLD BE WARNED

Sunday, February 28th, 2010.

The Americans scored with 24 seconds left in the gold medal game.

Stunned silence across Canada.

Jonathan Toews and Corey Perry scored the first two goals of the game for us and many people were assuming it was over. But give the Americans credit. They were a talented group that played with a lot of heart, and they battled back.

My wife Rene told me after the game that as disappointed as she was when the Americans scored, she didn't doubt the outcome would be in our favour. She described her mindset as an "eerie calm." She said she was inundated with text messages from friends "worried and frantic" at the turn of events. To which she texted back a singular and simple response:

"Keep the faith."

The truth is that if the Americans were going to score to tie it up, scoring with 24 seconds left probably saved us. Had they scored with three minutes left, the momentum swing would have made our task even tougher. The timing gave us a chance to get into the dressing room to regroup, reset, and refocus.

Going into overtime could have triggered doubt big time. Our confidence could have really been shaken. As a team, we weren't about to let that happen. Was there disappointment in our dressing room? Sure, but it didn't linger.

Was there any doubt?

No, absolutely not.

There may have been doubt out in the stands, in the streets of Vancouver, or in living rooms across the country. Inside the dressing room, the quiet but unmistakable confidence that had characterized our team was evident. We were ready. All of our hard work, dedication, and yes, the adversity we had faced had prepared us for this moment.

There was no way doubt was getting in the dressing room on that day.

Not during that game.

Not in that moment.

There are a lot of things you could say at big moments.

Entire books have been written on how to do it: how to inspire. The opportunity to bring together commitment, passion, and talent for breakthrough performance is something coaches and leaders in all walks of life obsess over.

The right words said in the right way for the desired impact. It's about directing emotion.

I try to be a straightforward guy. I want my words to paint a clear picture. I have always believed that the fewer the words, the clearer the picture. The best coaches put people in the right situations. You need to get people in the right roles and into the right mindset. If you know your players, if you understand your team, and if you have a real sense of the situation you're in, you've done due diligence. You're ready to go.

Bottom line, I say it as I see it.

The Olympic overtime would be played four-on-four, not five-on-five. So before we headed back onto the ice, I spoke about the technical side of how we would play it. Then I laid it out for the guys this way: "There's so much talent on the ice, this thing will be over quickly. In the next seven or eight minutes, one of you will be a hero for the rest of your life. It's time to put your foot on the gas and go after them."

Maybe Sidney Crosby paid attention to those words.

Some individuals, some teams are able to create their destiny. We were that kind of team. Difference-makers embrace big expectations.

They expect and will their performance to match the moment. Whether you're a doctor, lawyer, teacher, small business owner, or stay-at-home parent, your success is based on your ability to meet the moment.

You can't get caught up in the moment. You can't let it overwhelm you – staying focused and clear-headed is critical.

How you meet a moment can define success.

Some people believe the gold medal game was the greatest game in our hockey history.

We delivered in the biggest showcase, in the biggest game, at the biggest moment. I feel so privileged to have been a part of it.

One of the questions I get asked most often is "How did you handle the pressure?"

My answer is confidence. Confidence is key to handling pressure. Having previous experience, having learned from falling short, having built on success, having a track record over many championship opportunities, gives you the feeling you're going to deliver – the feeling that you're going to get the job done. If you have been through big-time situations before, you know what you can do. I think about confidence like a muscle. The more you exercise it, the stronger it gets. Cockiness or over-confidence can hurt you, but a well-honed confidence puts pressure in its proper place.

Confidence defines your perspective. Do you see opportunity or obstacle? Do you see possibility or problem? Do you see something to get excited about or be afraid of? Do you feel energized or tentative? Do you start doubting or start doing?

Confidence enables you to make strong choices.

Confidence helps you get beyond doubt.

Confidence gets you ready for big moments.

We had won that game before we hit the ice for overtime.

Champions know.

—·—·—

When Crosby scored the goal, my son Michael raised his arms, screamed at the top of his lungs, jumped over two rows of seats and slammed his entire body into the glass in celebration.

And an entire nation jumped for joy.

I knew at that moment, the parties I had hoped for would be happening all across Canada. People in every corner of the country would be celebrating hockey gold.

We had done our job. We had met expectations. We had fulfilled our potential.

We had created a moment that would be passed on for generations. People will come to ask, "Where were you when Sid scored the golden goal?"

It was the moment we had dreamed of as kids:

Arms raised.

Fists pumping.

Smiling from ear to ear.

Mobbed by his teammates.

The roar of the crowd.

A dream come true.

Sidney Crosby had scored a goal for the ages.

And kids all over Canada continue to dream.

What's the dream you're going to make happen?

CHAPTER 19

LEAVE NO DOUBT (PART TWO)

I started this book by saying the Leave No Doubt credo was a call to action. I said it was an approach that could help us achieve our dreams and make a difference. I told the story of how it came into being and I described the place it took in the dressing room during our journey toward winning Olympic gold.

That journey ended more than two years ago now. In retrospect, the credo feels more powerful than ever. And in the world we live in, it feels more important than ever to chase our dreams. I can tell you that I'm still out there chasing my dreams and trying to maximize my potential. Every day.

In the end, just know that the world is waiting for your best, your very best.

The world needs dream chasers.

So go ahead, get out in the world and inspire by doing.

Do good.

Do amazing.

Do impossible.

Do big.

Do small.

Do unexpected.

Do helpful.

Do inspirational.

Do meaningful.

Do different.

Do better.

Commit.

And feel free to warn the world you're coming. I believe in letting them know.

It's a promise you make to yourself.

Are you bringing the world the best you've got?

THE BABCOCK DICTIONARY

Accountability: doing your job

Activated: being mentally, physically, and emotionally focused

Adversity: a great opportunity that you're never happy to meet

Attitude: the unsung hero of being successful

Champions: those who dig deeper

Circle of Success: the process for continual improvement

Commitment: showing up in heart, mind, and body

Complacency: a feeling of comfort that encourages you to do nothing

Courage: the willingness to be honest with yourself and do what's necessary to get better

Doubt: the biggest thing standing between you and your dreams

Dreaming with your eyes open: everyday commitment

Dreams: things that seem impossible to everybody but you

Drive train: a person's will to succeed

Ego: an explosive energy that fosters confidence or selfishness

Family: your greatest source of pride and therefore deserving of your greatest commitment

Fear: a motivator only as effective as what you're afraid of

Foundation: the fundamental building blocks of a team's belief system

Gratitude: giving back

Heart: the capacity to go beyond what's physically possible

Humility: the genuine belief that you can always get better; a hunger to learn

Integrity: keeping the promises you make to yourself

Kitchen table accountability: a higher level of accountability coming from those who know you best

Leadership: serving your team's best interests

Losing: a textbook of lessons learned

Moment: a brief time that impacts a lifetime

Momentum: an invisible force that makes luck, good or bad, part of your team

Negativity: the biggest energy-taker there is

Ownership: making something part of who you are

Potential: the promise that keeps getting bigger as you get better

Preparation: the fuel needed to chase your dreams

Pressure: the feeling you get when you have a chance

Success: meeting your potential

Super-learners: people who work the direct line between preparation and excellence

Team: a group of individuals who find the power of their collective game

Winning: the one thing they can't take away from you

ACKNOWLEDGMENTS

Mike:

In these pages I've already extended my thanks to a lot of people, but I would especially like to thank my folks, Gail and Mike, my wife Rene, and my kids Allie, Michael, and Taylor. I'd also like to acknowledge Steve Yzerman and the management team for the greatest opportunity of my life outside of family. I want to thank the people of Hockey Canada led by Bob Nicholson along with the players, coaches, and support staff of Team Canada 2010. Without them, my family and I would not have had the chance to live our Olympic dream. And finally, thanks to the people of Canada for being so passionate about the game I love. Expressing that passion the way they did those fourteen days in February 2010 helped make it two weeks for the ages. No doubt.

Rick:

I would like to thank my family for their belief in chasing dreams. Thanks to my wife Gina and my daughters Annie and Grace for their day-to-day support, encouragement, and patience throughout the writing of this book. And thanks to my Dad for always being there. Thank you all for getting me past the "give-in" line.

We both thank the people at McGill-Queen's University Press for their guidance and input. Philip Cercone and Adrian Galwin were supportive of this project from the beginning. Mark Abley provided expert editing assistance.